PRAISE FOR *RIDING THE MAGIC CARPET*:

'Anyone on a quest must trade some degree of sanity for passion, and that's where the authenticity and adventurous charm of this book lies'   PLANET magazine

'His wonderful observations add humour and his uncanny ability to take the reader to some far flung wave heaven make this book a very worthwhile read indeed'   LINE UP surfing magazine

'Anderson includes an incredible depth and wealth of knowledge to an already dynamic surf adventure storyline'
                                                           FREEFLOW magazine

'... will appeal not merely to surfers but to fans of travel writing generally'   THE TIMES
'Awesome. It's not often that a book can get you as amped to travel as a good surf movie, but this one does!'
                                                     Matt Archbold, pro surfer

'Both adventurous and exciting... makes you dream about going on the ultimate surf safari'
                                         Kate Dendle, GB Women's Surf Team

'The extended road trip, for all its adrenaline and booze, bizarre locals and bureaucracy, is as much an insight into the drifter and dreamer's mentality as it is a surfer's guide'   SUNDAY EXPRESS

'If you've spent a lot of time travelling to surf, this book will bring back memories of a great many places – the experiences are real and the telling down to earth and genuine'   magicseaweed.com

GREY SKIES, GREEN WAVES

A SURFER'S JOURNEY AROUND THE UK AND IRELAND

TOM ANDERSON

summersdale

GREY SKIES, GREEN WAVES

Copyright © Tom Anderson, 2010

Map by Breige Lawrence

All rights reserved.

Summersdale Publishers Ltd
46 West Street
Chichester
West Sussex
PO19 1RP
UK

www.summersdale.com

Printed and bound by CPI Group (UK) Ltd, Croydon, CR0 4YY

ISBN: 978-1-84953-041-5

Substantial discounts on bulk quantities of Summersdale books are available to corporations, professional associations and other organisations. For details contact general enquiries: telephone: +44 (0) 1243 771107, fax: +44 (0) 1243 786300 or email: enquiries@summersdale.com.

CONTENTS

INTRODUCTION
A FRESH HOODOO

So this is surfing in Britain, I mused grumpily as I walked up a slope of wet rocks and wispy beach grass, trying to keep a foothold as rain and wind both tried their utmost to send me skidding back down to the freezing beach below. Another early morning dash down to the 'finest surf spot in Wales', another eager drive over the top of the headland at Freshwater West, anticipating great springtime waves – this was supposed to be the year I made a real go of this. And yes, only to be greeted by another sea of miserable wind-blown slop instead of the spectacular surf we'd all been hoping for. Another waste of petrol, even when they still went ahead with the event, another twenty-minute paddle against a rip – and for twelve more months I was doomed to kicking myself for yet again going out in the first round of the Welsh Nationals.

My mates were right. Why did I bother with this rigmarole, year after year?

Perhaps the longest and most irritating part of what was now becoming an annual tradition for me was the walk (or

7

trudge, perhaps) back from the water pondering what a fool I was for even trying. I knew the whole process off by heart now; riding in to shore lying down, the self-flattering excuses made in the face of the fellow competitors who'd beaten you fair and square, the pointlessly optimistic thought that maybe the result wasn't going to be the way you feared after all – all culminating in that climb back up the rocks to be greeted by a row of smug friends and spectators, all thoroughly amused at my latest humiliation – which had been confirmed over the tannoy moments before I arrived within earshot. It seemed me and the Welsh Nationals just weren't meant to be.

This particular year, though, I'd outdone even my own spectacular reputation as the 'first-round bomber' – heading the 200 yards or so down to the water's edge at low tide, through virtual gales and driving rain to surf abysmally in what was in fact not only the first round of the event but the very first *heat* of that very first round. Round one, heat one – and still it got worse. A no-show from the fourth man that would normally make up the numbers for a surf heat (who had obviously seen sense and stayed in bed) had ensured that it was a three-man affair – with two going through and one getting knocked out. This meant that, once I'd come third of three, I could lay claim merely twenty minutes into this year's Welsh National Surfing Championships to not only being one of a group of first-round bombers, but the *first* first-round bomber. A pioneer. A failure among failures! Of all the hundreds of people heading to Freshwater West that weekend to compete in the various categories on offer, I was, for the time it took to run heat two at least, the only person so far to have been eliminated from the event. My involvement in a three-day tournament had been so brief that I could have turned around, driven straight home and been back in the living room before *Saturday Kitchen* had even begun on the TV.

It was time to take stock of my life as a surfer in Britain, and to face some home truths.

In the past few years I'd loved surfing. No change there – as always, it was my reason for everything – but there had been one unfortunate caveat that was now coming back to bite me. I loved surfing *everywhere but the UK*. The act of riding a wave was becoming perhaps too synonymous for me with foreign travel. Great if you're away on trips all the time, but sooner or later that kind of hedonism catches up with you – and you get hooked on an unsustainable regime of wild, sun-beaten beaches, remote waves and no commitments. The trouble now was that this overindulgence in exotic surf-chasing had left me low on funds for a while and bereft of the passion needed to do anything useful as a surfer back home.

I'd often wondered why someone concerned only with that quest for adventure hadn't just emigrated – but things would never be that simple and I knew it. No journey would be a journey, if you catch my drift, if it didn't involve returning to a home of some kind, and for a while now I'd been trying to make more of being a surfer in Wales – or rather in Britain. I'd become too much of a snob, though, and it was getting harder to figure out how to turn it around.

However, there was one thing I could now be sure of: if I was going to get something out of my life as a British surfer then here at the Welsh Nationals I was surely barking up the wrong tree. As a kid I used to love packing for the long May bank holiday weekend in Pembroke, and always considered my own involvement in the contest second in importance to being present at the biggest celebration of national surfing that I knew of. Until the travel bug had got a hold of me. Now it felt like a pointless routine that I went through merely to keep myself on the map – to keep my name on the heat sheet.

And this year I'd barely even managed that.

By the time I'd found my car keys again (in the coat pocket of someone at contest control), turned my competitor's jersey back in to the beach marshal and read the hard copy of the result just for myself, that second wave of shame had started to come over me. However, it is often at these moments – and you'll know what I mean if you've ever competed in something serious – that you suddenly find an honesty and self-reflection that is rarely part of your thought processes.

'Surfers in heat three, get ready. Your paddle-out time starts in two minutes.' The announcer's voice over the speakers dulled my internal voice, but only for a moment.

This attitude and planned nonchalance towards coming here, I realised, was merely a safety mechanism. If I had a nightmare at the Welsh then it didn't matter because I could pretend not to care for the event and its waves anyway. (There was a hint of self-denial in this, given the fact it was usually held in surf that was easily as challenging as the stuff you'd ride abroad. Storm conditions appeared the norm at Freshwater West in May.)

The speaker, only a few yards from where I'd parked, jolted my senses again. 'Heat four, you should also be getting ready. Looks like the rain will be back by the time you get changed, too. Rather you than me!' Ah, the wit of surf-contest announcers.

Safety mechanism. That sounded like a big idea in a freezing, washed-out car park at nine in the morning when you've already been awake for nearly four hours. But it was true – and not only of the Welsh Nationals. I'd been harbouring an unfair cynicism for everything about surfing in Britain for a while now. This was a trick I kept playing on myself – the moaning and feeling constantly underwhelmed – and it was holding me back. Perhaps I'd been doing it to try and justify that wanderlust to go away again but, even so, it was time to can that nonsense for good. I needed to get out and about a bit more. At home, though; it was time to get to know my own backyard. It made perfect sense. Something was changing in me, for the better.

Now, it may have been my mood, my thoughts or it may have been luck (or, God knows, even fate), but little did I realise that the opportunity to start turning over this new leaf was going to present itself in the very next person I spoke to.

Usually at this point my routine was to get into the car the moment I was out of my wetsuit and into my layers of clothes again – before firing up the engine and driving away without another word to anyone. (A thoroughly satisfying act – for about thirty seconds before the third wave of shame hit.) Instead, however, through a gap in the drizzle, I found myself walking towards the infamous food and drinks van at the corner of Fresh West's car park – aptly named 'Snack Attack' – for a polystyrene coffee. *Sod it*, I thought, *why not stick around for five before doing a runner.*

In the queue was a friend from home, Elliot, who was in fact the European longboard champ and therefore entirely unfamiliar and unsympathetic with the plight of the first-round bomber. Always prepared and obviously at home here with his thick puffer-jacket, matching sponsor-branded beanie, year-round tan and once dark but permanently sun-tinted locks of curly hair, Elliot looked nothing like the man standing next to him. This man had a winter-white face adorned with expensive angular glasses and was dressed from head to toe in neatly pressed smart-casual office clothing. For once, here was someone who seemed more out of place at the Welsh than me. He looked slightly uneasy, even uptight, as if he'd never even been to a beach, which I learned was quite likely when Elliot introduced him as being from a London-based ad agency.

'Look at you, hanging out with ad men, ya ponce!' I wanted to say – half out of jealousy and half out of sincerity. But I didn't.

'Ad agency? What brings you down here?' I asked instead.

'Carl's down here looking for surfers to be in an ad he's making for the Welsh Tourist Board,' Elliot replied on his behalf.

'Yeah,' Carl nodded, wincing at the taste of his stewed and overheated tea. 'You keen? There's a free trip involved.'

'Really?' At this point my ears pricked up.

'Yeah. To North Wales. Ever been up there?'

For a moment the cynic in me tried to leap out, but then I saw where this could go.

'No. But I'm sure there's a first for everything.'

Carl looked at Elliot, who nodded back.

'Well, I'll pencil you in then,' he confirmed, reaching into his jacket pocket for a velvet notebook – an accessory that would last about twenty seconds in the rain. 'If you give me your details, I'll get back in touch...'

It's not often you think something up, only to see it start to happen immediately. This had to be a great sign. It was a starting point and the chance to try and discover the thrill of the journey without needing to get on a plane first. Maybe this could be the catalyst for a new-found love of the little island in the North Atlantic that I'd lived on for nearly thirty years without really learning to appreciate (and maybe even a few of the smaller islands that surround it too).

Not wanting to get carried away at such an early stage in an idea, mind, it wasn't long before I was back on the road home – but this time with something missing from the usual experience – that sense of hopelessness had gone. So I bombed out in the first round again... big deal. I'd been coming here for over fifteen years anyway – since being barely old enough to put my own wetsuit on – and this time it wasn't just bravado. It wasn't that I wouldn't love to get a result down there one day – it had merely slipped into perspective among other priorities, other ideas. With each mile my life as a British surfer was suddenly regaining purpose.

I began remembering my other journeys home from the Welsh – and I even smirked at the times I'd sped, utterly dejected, along this stretch of road. Not since the Under 20s category nearly a decade ago had this journey been made with any silverware in hand. But did that really matter? Friends used to joke about the Nationals, bombarding me with such witticisms as, 'Off to the Welsh tomorrow, eh? I'll see you back home at lunchtime then!'

I wondered what positive side effects a firm plan to start wandering the British Isles might have on my surfing – perhaps it was the missing ingredient for this kind of event anyway. All about the way you approach something. The guys who did well on these weekends in the cold all loved what they were doing – that was key. They were stoked on British surfing, subscribers to every aspect of it – faithful for better or for worse.

In the not-too-distant future, I vowed, that would be me. I would return here one day, ready to enjoy the experience again. And to rediscover this stoke I'd go wherever I needed in the British Isles. This journey could begin in a few weeks' time, by meeting Carl and Elliot in North Wales.

It didn't take long to realise how much fun this might turn out to be. Something you can't avoid when you decide to get out and about along Britain's coasts is the sheer unpredictability of the people you'll meet and the situations you'll end up in – and this was going to be no exception. You take it for granted abroad, but there's something special about getting out of your comfort zone and discovering the thrill of the road in your own country.

Two weeks later, as the first small stage of a bigger plan was coming together, I was on the phone to Carl and getting the brief. It was sounding interesting already...

'We'll meet you in the B & B in Pwllelli tomorrow night. The other surfers are all going to be there too. Get some sleep when you arrive, OK? We need to get to Hell's Mouth early the next morning. The director's bringing the sheep up overnight.'

'You what?' Had I just heard him right?

'The sheep,' Carl repeated. 'Your co-stars. The producer's fetching them overnight. You'll see what I mean when you get there. *Hwyl fawr.*'

And the phone clunked dead.

My journey through Britain and Ireland's surf cultures was getting underway with the 'North Wales Wild Sheep Chase'. A fittingly unpredictable start…

CHAPTER 1
A NORTH WALES WILD SHEEP CHASE

'*Bendigedig!*'

Surely of all the weird and wonderful words thrown up by my supposedly native tongue, this has to be my favourite. It means 'wonderful', and sounds, well… wonderful – especially when you hear it in a North Walian, or 'Gog' accent. As if Welsh wasn't already a supremely challenging language to learn, it becomes utterly indecipherable all over again when spoken by the Gogs. Except for that one word, which had just been said through a big smile by the old lady in Pwllelli who ran the B & B Carl had put me and my three other travel partners up in.

For me it represented a double whammy of stoke. Not only was it the first word I'd recognised since arriving in the Gog, but it was also her response to being told that tomorrow morning we planned to go surfing at first light. This statement could often be greeted with a look of disdain in many other parts of the UK, but here it seemed fine. Breakfast could be ready whenever we wanted, she explained, it made no difference to her.

'Aha – *bendigedig*,' I grinned back, feeling pleased with myself, at last only a yawn away from a comfortable bed.

After one of the most gruelling drives in living memory, we had arrived somewhere.

You may wonder, from looking at a map of the British Isles – home of the smooth motorway and careful driver – why a distance as comparatively short as South to North Wales could take so long to drive. It does, though, I can assure you. It takes an absolute age.

This is partly due to the fact that the A470, Wales's version of perhaps the English M6, the French A10 or the US's I-90, turns to a winding single-lane plod over hills and farm country about thirty miles north of Cardiff – which often means spending hours at a time in a tractor-related tailback. The knock-on effect of this is the other reason it's such a tough trip: because of the A470's inadequacies, you could probably type the same destination into a satnav and get a different route each time. There is, quite simply, no official quickest way.

And this means getting lost. Often.

Naturally, in our case, that event had befallen us before we'd even covered half of the distance north as the crow flies, which was some time not too long after midday. Not that this mattered much. It was a predicament that delighted me. Only a few hours in to this plan to rediscover the joys of surf-tripping at home and I had been joyfully reassured of something very important: at least you *could* get lost in Wales!

'Well, there are three roads heading north,' said Dan Harris, a longboarder from Aberafan and my co-pilot. Pushing a lock of blonde hair behind his right ear and unfolding a corner of his damp road atlas, he turned to the other two in the back for extra approval, 'But I couldn't tell you which one is quickest. The thickest line is the longest but the direct one looks kind of, you know, like a lane.'

The sun was just starting to peek out from behind a few clouds as we sat in the car park of Sainsbury's in Aberystwyth, all keen to work out whether or not we were making progress.

In the rear seats – assigning the boards to the roof – were the other two people Carl had booked for this seemingly unorthodox photoshoot. One was Elliot, of course, and the other his girlfriend Nia – a medical student he'd met at uni in Cardiff. Elliot (or 'Smelliot' as he was known to friends) had perhaps the best life imaginable. He was a part-time student and a part-time pro longboarder. He could opt in and out of either role as and when he fancied, or needed. When necessary, he could skip important events on the university calendar (of which there were very few anyway, as he studied French and Spanish) by simply explaining to his lecturers that he *had* to go to the Maldives, Taiwan, Costa Rica, South Africa, California – wherever his pro-surfer life required. Similarly, though, if a contest or photo trip was somewhere he didn't feel like going, he could play the 'unmissable exam' or 'urgent deadline' card to his sponsors.

But for some inexplicable reason, North Wales had escaped such excuses.

'Got to get to know our own country, eh?' he explained. 'And also, I heard from a mate who did something with these guys and he says they're pretty wacky.'

As our link to Carl, the guy organising the whole thing, Elliot was supposed to be the person in the know. If he was, though, he was keeping tight-lipped about it.

'All he's told me is it's in Hell's Mouth and there are sheep involved.'

'And longboards,' I moaned. So far that was my only reservation. Dan, Elliot and Nia were all longboarders – riding boards over nine feet in length – although Dan did have a shortboard on the roof as well, for emergencies. For him, the longboard thing was quite new. He and I used to be rivals as grommets (the nickname for a kid surfer), both on shortboards, and had lined up for the Welsh junior team together. This was in the days before he discovered a knack for longboarding, and since then he had found considerable success. In fact, the only longboarder in Wales more decorated than him was, to his great annoyance, Elliot.

As for Nia, well, I'd never been on a surf trip of any kind with her before – but as she was also a longboarder there was already a sense that the odd one out on this trip was me. Although I didn't mind that – all it did was add to the feeling I was opening up new horizons; ones broken by the striking mountain ranges of North Wales.

Bendigedig!

The last half-hour of those mountains had passed us by at night, but I'd still been able to feel the acute turns and drops in the road.

Now arrived, the sea air ensured that it was with that comforting feeling of journey's end that we walked out of our B & B in search of Carl and a place to eat.

Over a curry, we were talked through the details of the shoot – but they were still sketchy.

'I don't really know what Ivan's got in mind,' he explained, a slightly vacant look on his face. 'I just organise the people. This is what I do. I'm given a list of what they need and then it's off to find the right faces.'

This, I learned, was what had brought him to the Welsh Nationals.

'For this ad it was three male surfers and one female, so I figured Fresh West for the National Championships was the best place to find that.'

'Gosh. You're sharp,' Dan quipped.

'Yeah. Tell me about it. But it wasn't as straightforward as that. There was another part to this order, which I haven't had to do before. I only specialise in people, see. But they wanted two sheepdogs and nine sheep, too.'

This was our chance to quiz him on the involvement of sheep. You had to be slightly worried – a London ad agency, Wales, sheep, surfers. Something gave me the feeling a few of the classic stereotypes were going to get wheeled out in the morning.

'You're not gonna make a bunch of knobs out of us are you?' Dan promptly asked, merely voicing what the rest of us were thinking. He nudged Elliot. 'Smelliot here has got a public image to protect, see. He wants to get into the modelling thing once he's too far over the hill for longboarding.'

Elliot frowned. 'Shut up, Harris.'

'Well that's gonna be a while,' I ventured. 'Longboarders over the hill? It's an old man's sport anyway, isn't it?'

Nia laughed. The others ignored me. Elliot turned back to Carl and asked the same question in a more polite tone, 'Seriously, though, d'you know why they wanted sheep?'

Carl drained his wine glass and shook his head.

'Nope. We'll have to wait until the morning. See you at breakfast. We'll need to be at the beach by eight. They need to catch it while the shoreline's backlit. That's the only other thing I know.'

And with that he paid the bill, and left us to it.

If a B & B is to be judged by its breakfasts, which in the UK they often are, then this Pwllelli guest house got North Wales off to a great start the next morning.

Although Elliot, ever the consummate pro, took the continental option, the 'full Welsh' on offer was just perfect to line your stomach the morning after a long drive and a generous curry. In other words it was starchy, heavy and big. To top things off, it came with a gigantic pot of coffee that was so strong you got the shakes only halfway through the first mug. All in all about as inappropriate a start to a day's surfing as you could hope for – but for Dan, Nia and me it was ideal. We still didn't know to what extent the actual act of surfing would be required of us anyway – and when someone else (Carl) is paying, it's rude not to gorge yourself.

So full that it was hard not to fall back asleep, we set off on the fifteen-minute journey to the nearby beach at Hell's Mouth.

Hell's Mouth is a vast stretch of white sandy beach on the very tip of the Llŷn Peninsula. It reaches out, narrow and bold, from the rest of Wales's landmass, extending tentatively towards Ireland's east coast. Lying at the northernmost extreme of the turbulent Cardigan Bay and able to pick up swells from way out in the Atlantic, it has a reputation for being wild, barren, feisty and, as South Wales marched headlong towards becoming a succession of cities and shopping malls, reassuringly hostile – which is what you'd expect from a place called Hell's Mouth. To the north are a series of deep green headlands that rise sharply out of the sea, a reminder of the mountainous nature of so much of North Wales. With crystal clear water running quickly into a horizon of imposing dark blue, the place is definitely photogenic. It presents itself as commanding and untouched by any significant human development. I could see why we were here.

On this particular morning, the beach was in receipt of an enormous swell. After shaking hands with Ivan, the cameraman from the ad agency, we trudged over the dunes to discover walls of white water rolling majestically towards the beach. As each row of churning, pearl-white foam bounced its way through the line-up it would simply be replaced by another. Here and there, across the four-mile-long beach, you could make out wave sections that would be incredible to surf – if you could get out there and put yourself in place for one.

That, however, would be a huge test.

With nothing but a long stretch of featureless beach each side of us, there were no rip-currents to help a surfer paddle out, and no defined sandbanks to hold peaks in place. And yet the light onshore winds were crumbling the wave faces, causing them to chop up and break with no real sequence. The waves weren't closing out (meaning they were breaking across the beach without peeling properly), and putting together any sort of show for Ivan, who was eagerly loading his camera gear onto his back, would require submitting ourselves to a workout not dissimilar to that of a heavyweight boxer in the run-up to a world-title fight. Man, or woman, against ocean.

Despite this, Elliot, feeling the carbs from his own high-and-mighty breakfast choice (which was now clearly an example of the wise decision-making that had helped him to the top), was mad for it. Eyes wide with the thrill of the challenge, he approached Ivan.

'What's the plan then? Are we in there?'

'Oh, yes, yes. Definitely,' came the reply the rest of us were dreading. 'How long does it take you to assemble your equipment for surfing?'

'Er, not long, like...'

'Half an hour?'

'Nah. We could be in there in five or ten minutes.'

Speak for yourself, I wanted to cut in, dopey with the weight of my breakfast.

'Oh, OK. Maybe wait a few minutes then. There's been a delay with the sheep.'

Trying to hide my relief, I wondered if Ivan could finally be the one to explain to us the nature of this project we had signed up for.

He could.

'Well, what we've got is a concept from copywriting and a bit of a sketch. It's part of that ad campaign – you know it? "Wales: The Big Country"?'

'Yeah, I know it.'

'This one's the last of the series now – we've done the other ones.' He sat against the open boot of his Volvo estate and pulled out a small plastic portfolio. 'Have a look.'

He opened it up and started flicking through, settling on a page somewhere towards the back. A collection of 'great outdoors'-type shots had been coupled with slogans befitting the front page of the *Mirror* – which was a style of writing I'd always had great reverence for. Snappy, witty, filled with puns and triple- or even quadruple-meanings.

A photo showed two hikers at the foot of Snowdon looking upwards, with the caption 'Area of outstandingly bad mobile reception'.

There were other ads in there too: one of an ice cream van marooned in the middle of a beach, without a slogan as yet, and another of an aerial shot of a coastal golf course being buffeted by wind, with a scorecard containing stupidly high shot-counts – 9, 8, 9, 10, 7, 8 – and a handwritten note saying 'but loving it'.

And then he showed us the very back of the folder, which had the same ads but in sketch form – in light pencil, with crude pastel lines over the top. They were surprisingly accurate to the finished image – even though the sketches had obviously come first. I knew that was the mark of a great photographer; to imagine a picture and then be able to source its setting and take it as a real-life image with little change from the original plan.

But he was going to have his work cut out here.

He pulled out the sketch that was today's blueprint. For a start, the waves in his image were much smaller than the great barriers of water we'd be squaring up to today.

Their idea was neat, though. A sheep was standing in the foreground, looking out to sea, while in the centre of the image a surfer raced their way across the bay. The detail was as tight as in the others. The beach was clearly Hell's Mouth. The perspectives were rigidly numbered with even lighter pencil, explaining at exactly what depth of focus each layer was to be shot. And the slogan?

Oh dear.

It read: 'Beware! The Great Woolly Whites.'

Nice.

But, unfortunately, as is the perennial problem when you marry surfing and the mainstream media, the artist's concept of the act of wave riding was skewed to the point of insult. The surfer had obviously been drawn by someone who knew nothing about it. Standing in some kind of ninja pose about a foot from the nose of a water craft resembling an ironing board, he was hanging coolly in the curl – essentially pulling what looked like a never-ending floater (a manoeuvre that involved sliding along the roof of the breaking wave – and one you'd be lucky to hold for more than a second or two). The predicament indicated in Ivan's picture was gravitationally impossible – and that's being kind. It was the kind of misconception that often happens in kids' cartoons, where SpongeBob, Lilo and Stitch, Scooby Doo et al suddenly find themselves poised perfectly in the most deadly part of a stationary wave, whooping as it moved nowhere, simply throbbing on the spot. At least they weren't hoping for any wipeouts.

I looked out to sea as another mountain of water burst and bludgeoned its way across the bay. I realised how small surfing's vocabulary was. I'd have just called it big and blown out. But woolly whites seemed a pretty good description – if not a little happy-go-lucky – to capture the exact nature of the ordeal we were about to go through to create an idyllic snapshot of the great Welsh outdoors. Still, I logged the term. Woolly whites. I had to try and use it again some time. 'What's the surf like, mate?' 'Two foot. Lined up. Woolly whites for sure, man.'

It crossed my mind for a moment that Ivan had probably never really watched the sea before. Knowing its movements and patterns was something I'd always taken for granted – having spent most of my life not much further than a few miles from a shoreline.

Carl's phone rang and he answered it loudly, interrupting my train of thought.

'Hello? Yeah. Yeah it is, mate. Yeah I know. Yeah they are. Right here. Yeah we're all ready. OK. See you in a minute.'

He clipped his phone shut and turned to us, shoving his hands in his pockets.

'They're about two minutes away. Director's worrying about the light. Wants to get as much shooting time as possible, so he's wondering if you can get ready. If you were in the water when he got here that'd be ideal. Apparently the sheep are a bit wound up, and the sheepdogs, too. They'll have never been to the beach before. They live on a farm in mid-Wales, see. Anyway, he reckons they won't have that long and if they can just release the sheep straight away with you guys in there it'd be pretty helpful.'

The sheep and dogs had been driven up overnight. Apparently it would minimise disruption to their owner if they could go straight onto the beach and then back in the trailer to head home again.

'The nearest place we could hire this kind of sheep for the shoot was St Clears in Pembroke, see,' Carl explained.

'What? That's by Fresh West,' I noted.

'Yeah, that's right. It had to be one type of sheep in particular, though. The *Lleyn* it's called. They're local to around here, which makes it kind of annoying that we have to bring them up from bloody south-west Wales. But that's the kind of thing that happens when you do my job. Had to be *Lleyns*, though. It's the one Dom had in mind when he thought of the concept.'

'Dom?'

'The director,' Ivan cut in. 'He's not here yet. He's a genius, man. Quiet guy. Won't have a lot to say himself. Leaves that to us. I'll tell you what to do.'

The thought of Ivan telling us how to surf made even Elliot, now halfway into his wetsuit, chuckle quietly.

'Did Dom come up with "woolly whites" then?' I asked.

'Of course, man,' Ivan beamed. 'Great, innit.'

Trying to ignore the kilo of egg, sausage and bacon sloshing around in my belly, I reached for my wetsuit, which was still damp as it was used far too often to dry out properly, and started getting in the mood for a real battle. This surf was going to need a lot of energy.

Dan was debating whether to ride his short or longboard, and decided to solicit Ivan's advice.

'The long one will show up better on the picture,' the now ready photographer mumbled, obviously not really having an opinion on the matter.

As we set off over the dunes to the desolate stretch of beach, the only surfers in sight (which with a good swell running was a clear sign that somewhere else was probably firing right now), I heard the sound of a clunking engine and barking dogs. The sheep and their entourage were arriving. This was how I imagined it to be when you are working on a film set with a demanding and tardy movie star that suddenly shows up and steals everyone's attention. Suddenly Carl, who had been walking with us, turned and ran back – instantly diverting his fickle energy to the real stars of the show. I wondered if the sheep were actually aware of how important they were today. Wales's frontline fight for tourists' cash was in their hands – sorry – hooves.

From their point of view, however, it was just a scary day out, getting chased around by snarling sheepdogs in a landscape of sand and salt air that might as well be the surface of Mars for all they knew.

We'd reached the water's edge, and I looked out to sea at ominous, towering walls of water. It was time to focus.

Elliot was super-keen. I could see determination in his eyes as he shook any remaining stiffness out of his shoulders, readying himself to do what he did best. Similarly, the other two were both thinking only about getting on with surfing. This, I realised, was the point where usually I would start to grumble – if only to myself – about the cold, the wind, the constant irritations of surfing in Britain. But that was something I'd come here to confront. There existed more than one way of seeing things. Sure, in front of me was a cold, uninviting sea of choppy, inconvenient surf – if I chose to see it that way. But there was also an exhilarating tussle with the powers of the North Atlantic on offer, the reward potentially being the chance to rev across some big waves at high speeds. All I had to do was drag myself a half-mile or so out to sea to be in place to catch one of them.

Ignore trepidations and get on with it, I ordered myself. *Enjoy being out of your comfort zone. You would if you were anywhere else.*

The water felt a little warmer than Porthcawl – part of the Gulf Stream making its way almost directly up this way. It was mid-spring, so you still felt the sharp change in temperature on your feet and hands as land turned to ocean. And then came the first duck-dive. I sunk my board and plunged downwards after it to slip under the oncoming wave, a little shiver went through my head as it too adjusted to the new surroundings. I resurfaced awake and fresh, taking a gulp of air and digging in for the paddle out.

Ten, twenty and then thirty duck-dives later, red-faced and shoulders filling with lactic acid, I sat up on my board. I was about halfway out – with no sign of the other three anywhere. There must have been a trough in the sandbanks below as I'd found a little patch of water that seemed not to have any breaking waves. Back on the beach I could now see several figures running around, chasing sheep and dogs in all directions. Another three people were standing on a dune, either watching passively or waiting to get involved themselves. I wondered if one was Dom, the mysterious director of the shoot. The one whose imagination had turned what was going on all around me into 'woolly whites'.

I needed to keep paddling for their sake as much as mine. Momentarily rested, I took aim and prepared for the final push towards the almost mythical zone of calm water that I knew existed somewhere beyond the immediate foreground of angry white water – or wool as the Welsh Tourist Board planned to soon dub it.

When you're in the middle of a big swell, the horizon can often be hidden by rising and breaking water – and on a particularly tough paddle-out it can be hard to gain perspective of how far you are from where you need to be. Using the beach as a marker though, I knew the end of this watery treadmill had to arrive soon.

Eventually a gap between sets appeared, and I dashed for it, throwing every drop of power in my shoulders towards the goal of making it to the line-up.

When I got there, I saw Elliot waiting, relaxed, for the right wave.

'Where are the others?' I asked.

'Dunno,' he said, dismissively. 'I think Harris just caught one. Not sure.'

As he said this, we both started paddling again when we saw a solid set approaching just to our south. Ahead of me, and a few seconds quicker with his paddling, I saw Elliot lock in to the first wave. He looked quickly up and down the beach both ways, working out whether to take off to the right or left. The wave lifted just as it got to him, rising up into a thick peak, and Elliot jumped to his feet and dropped in.

He was gone. I couldn't see what happened to him from there, other than knowing that he made the take-off. Neither could I see whether Ivan had been able to take any shots of him from the shoreline. All these things were peripheral to the fact that a second wave was also heading into the line-up within my range, if I paddled quickly enough.

As it neared and I kicked my feet at the water behind, I could already feel I was going to be able to catch it. There was power in this swell – that feeling of being able to surf with speed at your disposal. I jumped up and turned towards the right and onto a wide, rolling wave face. Moving this fast you could feel an instant response to any change in weight or balance. I tried to put my board on its edge – or 'rail' – as deftly as possible, using my speed to redirect back towards the steeper pocket of the wave, reaching the bottom again just as a long wall rose in front of me. At the end of it was a huge bump of white water (or wool), pouring across the unbroken part. Glancing off it, I angled back towards the left again – to see the entire wave reform and stack up all over again. I was still at least fifty yards away from the beach, and this was already a screamer of a ride.

When I eventually bashed my way off the last section, now only a stone's throw from the shoreline, I could see Ivan running towards me, camera in hand. He was waving frantically. Before I could respond with any kind of gesture, he suddenly turned, dropped onto his knee and aimed his camera at an oncoming trio of sheep. He fired off a load of shots as they ran past him. At the end of my ride, I sunk into the shallows and got back on to my board. Whether I'd still been riding anything as the sheep passed would be down to luck rather than any surfer-photographer teamwork.

The second paddle out was infinitely easier, having just ridden one of my best British waves of the year so far. Where was this kind of form when I'd needed it during the Welsh a few weeks ago?

When I reached the line-up this time I was granted a little longer to puff and pant before a set came. I used the time to look back at the beach, where it looked as though the sheep were running riot. The dogs were nowhere to be seen and poor Ivan had dug himself into a dune, lying on his stomach with his lens trained like a sniper on the farce unfolding in front of him. The only thing missing was *The Benny Hill Show* theme tune for comedic effect.

Not my problem, I decided. My selfish surfer persona had taken hold.

Four waves later I was again sitting out back – by now feeling pretty pleased with myself and buzzing from the vigour of it all. Here and there I'd glimpsed the others, either paddling or riding, before eventually spotting Elliot walking up the beach.

I took a quick ride on a smaller wave, which only took me a little of the way in, and paddled back out to find Dan sitting where I'd just taken off.

'Getting a couple?' I asked.

'Fuckin' right. There are some steaming waves in here, man. I just had one that was like Sunset Beach, like!'

'What's Smelly doing?'

'Dunno. Might go in and see, like. They won't be taking any more pics if he's not in here. We're not good-looking enough.'

I laughed.

I love the vanity of surfers. We were both right in the middle of a classic session and yet all it took to get us back on the sand was the thought that Ivan might have stopped taking our picture. As soon as Dan had said that we both took waves to the beach where Nia had also made her way up the sand and was sitting next to Ivan, who, sure enough, did appear to have packed up.

On seeing us making our way to the shore, he stood up slowly and began walking towards us. Convinced this apparent nonchalance was down to his having taken a million great photos of us charging across the woolly whites behind, I smiled and gave him a thumbs up and raised my eyebrows to gesture a question.

He didn't respond.

'How'd we do?' Dan asked.

'You get much?' I added.

'Uh, no. I haven't taken one picture yet.'

'You *what*?'

'I haven't been able to take one. You're all surfing too far out.'

'Really?'

'Yeah. Can you stay a bit closer to the shore, please?'

This made sense. The biggest of the waves were breaking a long, long way from the shoreline – enough to make you feel as if you were halfway to Ireland when sitting out there.

'OK,' I replied. 'How close? What's good for you?'

'Much, *much* closer,' he said sternly. Behind him I could see Elliot looking forlorn.

'OK. That we can do. How far then – you point out.'

'About five metres from the sand?'

The two of us stared at him, dumbstruck, before looking in unison back at the creeping shoreline.

'Five metres?'

'Or closer.'

Dan tried to explain that it would be physically impossible to ride a wave that close to the sand. Not only would our fins drag along the bottom but there would be no power to keep you afloat.

Little did we know that Elliot had already tried telling Ivan this and that the whole shoot had been thrown into jeopardy by these Londoners not knowing enough about surfing.

Elliot was talking to Dom, the director, a gaunt man with jet-black hair in a long ponytail and purple denim trousers. I walked over to them, discovering that he spoke so softly you couldn't hear his voice unless you got to about a foot away.

'I'm going to talk it over with Ivan,' he was saying.

Right now, this appeared to be one of the silliest situations I'd ever gotten myself into during all my time as a surfer. We were being told to stay within five metres of the beach in order to allow a photographer to keep his camera focused on a sheep.

'They should have booked a surf school to do this for them,' Elliot quipped. 'They stay only a few metres from the sand.'

'Must be pretty hard, though,' Nia said, defending the now absent Ivan, who had walked off for a tête-à-tête with Dom. 'Keeping those things in focus,' she pointed at a stray sheep that had come to take a look at us, 'while trying to get a shot of one of us riding a wave.'

I sat in the sand and stared at the sheep. Mesmerised, like a newborn baby, it just gazed back at me, its entire psyche clearly focussed solely on trying to work out what the hell I was. A line of thin water swept its way gradually up the beach, catching the sheep's hooves, which caused it to jump on the spot and trot away – all memories of the strange wetsuited creature probably already wiped from its sieve-like mind.

Ivan was returning. And he didn't look happy.

'OK. I'm going to have to change focus. It's not cool at all, because the picture's going to look nothing like the sketch now.'

I was struggling to see why this really mattered, but apparently it did. Clearly not being able to reproduce a photographic likeness of a drawing was a first for Ivan, and one that made me feel a growing sense of pride at the awkwardness of surfing and surfers.

'You'll be able to go to twenty-five yards out now,' he frowned 'That any better?'

It wasn't much better, truth be told, but by now we were all starting to want out of this increasingly odd situation. The only way to do that would be to try and ride a few waves within the generously increased range he'd just outlined.

Of course, what followed was indeed a farce of the highest order. With a six-foot-two shortboard, designed to ride across fast, unbroken waves, I promptly set about trying to catch small lumps of shoreline dribble – waves that a surf school on big buoyant beginners' crafts would indeed make much better use of. Next to me was the European longboard champion, also standing, a picture of humiliation, on waves a few inches high and routinely riding them directly towards the beach. The great Elliot was getting back to basics.

At least he had a longboard – a board that made this kind of surfing possible. For me, it was never going to happen. I'd catch a small wave, jump up and then get the chance to pump my board a few times before it would sink beneath me.

And all the while the session was taking place to a soundtrack of barking sheepdogs and their baying owner, the farmer from mid-Wales – who had come dressed for the beach in his wellies, dai cap and tweed jacket. Lying behind them was Ivan, once again belly-down in the wet sand like a frontline soldier. He kept disappearing from view as a cloud of alarmed sheep passed him again and again – being driven in circles by the two dogs.

Woolly whites all around me, I thought. If the tourist board couldn't convince the general public to fall back in love with the Wales through this display, then there would be no hope.

They were winning me over, at least.

Once our humiliation on the sands of Hell's Mouth was finally over and Ivan had triumphantly declared that he'd scored the shot we needed, the ad agency offered to feed us again. As is common sense when offered a free lunch, we accepted. This meant a trip to a pub in the nearby town of Abersoch – a humble beachside settlement with a harbour tucked warmly behind the eastern flank of the Llŷn's exposed tip. It had a surf shop and winding streets with neat houses and salt air. Although no doubt heavily reliant on tourists in the height of summer, Abersoch's lack of chain logos and obvious sales pitches made it seem sure of its identity as a beach town on the end of a peninsula in the furthest corner of the least-populated home nation. But then most places with surf often do have that sort of self-confidence – that knowledge that, whatever else, they hold paramount, year-round significance to a dedicated tribe of followers.

Since someone else was paying, we all ordered the most expensive thing on the menu – a large steak – along with a pint of the Purple Moose Brewery's *Cwrw Madog*, the local ale. We followed it with dessert, and promptly all began falling asleep right there in the dimly lit pub lounge. The contrast between this warm shelter and the windswept beach that had preceded it was hitting us, along with fatigue from the demanding surf and the drive up yesterday.

Half an hour or so lapsed, during which time Ivan and Dom said thanks, paid us and got us to sign all sorts of forms before heading off – presumably to London to go and analyse their images of woolly whites.

Drowsy and in danger of warming up too much to ever want to go back in the water, it was Dan who ruthlessly called us back into action. The good swell yet lack of other surfers at the beach had been a sign there were probably great waves breaking somewhere else in this vicinity. It was now our mission to find them. We had to get up and out, and soon.

This was the pay-off. Now free from our modelling obligations, it was time to turn the rest of the afternoon into pure surf trip.

The only one of us who had been here before, Dan, claimed to know already where we had to go.

'Porth Ceriad!' he stated unequivocally. 'Big, barrelling lefts. There's tons of swell today, so I reckon it'll be breaking.' He was referring to a series of heavy and hollow lefts that broke off a cliff headland. I'd seen shots of it in surf mags before, usually with a surfer hanging out of the lip, poised perilously halfway between doom and glory. Porth Ceriad had a reputation for steep drops and explosive, bouncing peaks.

Sharp of mind when he needed to be, Dan could remember the way there too.

We headed back out of Abersoch in the direction we'd come, but this time turned left along a quick succession of lanes, until an approaching cliff indicated we'd found the west coast again.

When we pulled up it was obvious Dan's call had been spot-on. Several cars were parked up, their boots open with surfers either changing into or out of wetsuits in the space behind. You could see from their faces that the surf was good. Those with wet hair looked satisfied, stoked, while the ones that were getting ready to go in carried looks of anticipation and eagerness.

A light mist, barely perceptible, was drifting up from the beach, which was some way below us. When I walked to the edge of the sloping path down, a row of cleanly defined peaks each stacked up and broke mechanically. The wind that had carried an awkward direction for Hell's Mouth was now lightly grooming the waves. There was a headland over to our left from which the lines were refracting. You could see each row of energy moving through the ocean's surface, before criss-crossing off of the headland and rising up to pitch forward at the point of overlap. From this elevated position it brought a new clarity to the term 'A-frame' (where the water is decorated with rows of symmetrical, wedging wave patterns, each mimicking the shape of the letter 'A' itself).

The way the peaks rolled away from the headland meant the waves were mostly what we'd call 'lefts' or 'left-handers'. With us being 'natural foots' (or 'regular foots') – we stood on a wave with our left feet forward – this meant we'd be surfing with our backs to the unbroken faces, known as 'backhand' or 'backside'.

'I'm getting my shortboard this time,' Dan announced. 'Steep lefts – got to be done.'

You couldn't really judge the height of the waves from what was almost a bird's eye view of the beach – but I knew these would be challenging waves to ride well on a longboard. Elliot would manage to make it look easy though, no doubt.

Sure enough, this was an accurate prediction. As we descended from car park to beach, the front-on perspective began to emerge. The swell was running at just over head-height, with some bigger sets. And most of the waves were breaking fast, steep and powerful, pitching from top to bottom in one smooth motion. I watched lip after lip lurch forward, a crisp cracking sound echoing each time around the surrounding cove on impact. With a cumbersome nine-footer like Elliot's, merely fitting the curve of the board into that rapidly changing wave face or pocket would require balance, precision and strength.

Elliot pulled all of this off with panache and an apparent absence of any effort. Surfers often talk about the idea of 'grace under pressure', and this was exactly what we were treated to from the moment he paddled out at Porth Ceriad. On a heavy board that under the feet of most would have done entirely its own thing, he glided his way through tight sections and late drops, deftly making slight yet precise adjustments to his feet and body position.

I'd paddle over wave after wave, seeing the shoulder bend in, horseshoe-shaped – and each time Elliot would manage to get in and out of the lip as quickly as most shortboarders. I'd see him, Dan, Nia or one of the other four surfers in the water drop in and angle across the steep faces, until a shower of wind spray lifted off the breaking lip, blinding me, masking whatever else was going on.

The intense nature of the ride here at Porth Ceriad made it a very private experience. We'd sit in the line-up waiting, talking to each other – sharing the session – until a wave came along. From there a few yards of paddling would be all it took to drop a world away from the serenity of the line-up and into a grinding peak.

With the waves bending in towards you immediately from take-off, predicting the movement of the lip was very hard; although Elliot seemed able to do it by using that sixth sense that some surfers are gifted with.

After slipping down a solid wave myself and scraping to hold on, I found myself careering towards an oncoming section. The power under my feet was a rare sensation – that bliss of feeling the perfect line on a wave that is stacking up exactly as you want it to. Blessed for a moment with the exact sense of what to do, I jumped down from a floater to land metres from the shore, kicking out just in time to avoid running aground. Behind me a lull between waves had temporarily calmed the sea. I paddled back out, energised by the feeling I'd just had – the wind in my hair as I raced across the wave, the responding board under my feet, water drawing up the wave face, transferring its power through my body. Around me was the light crackling of white foam left by the wave I'd ridden, as a gentle backwash helped carry me back towards where the others were floating, each completely absorbed with the swell North Wales had given us.

'How was that one, Anderson?' Elliot asked. 'Some sick ones out here, eh? Should have seen Harris on that last one, too. This is what it's about.'

'So you wouldn't rather be abroad somewhere?' I asked him.

'Why? This is pumping.'

Dan nodded in agreement.

Already, just one trip in, I was getting more from British surfing than I remembered being possible. This was close to the eagerness I'd felt when first catching the bug as a teenager.

Conversation halted, as we drifted around the line-up. The sea was resetting itself, preparing for another series of thumping waves.

I knew that this evening, as night fell, I would be driving home with that feeling of a warm, sun- and wind-beaten face, the salty skin and aching shoulders: all the welcome side effects of a day saturated with surfing.

The others were right. Why would I want to change this for anything else?

That moment back at the Welsh had been every bit as significant as I'd hoped. This was exactly what I needed to be doing more of. Of course surf stoke was alive and well in the British Isles. I just needed to venture away from the backyard for something other than a contest from time to time in order to find my own slice of it.

I thought now about that morning back at Fresh West and realised something had happened to me since. I'd lost the sense of resentment. I started to recall other times from an age long ago when I'd wanted to go to a contest, or dashed along a motorway on a freezing day in search of swell. And then it occurred to me: I wanted that stuff again. The youngster who would awaken bouncing with anticipation to get out and about on the British surf scene had never left, and now it was time to catch up with him all over again.

Looking at the other surfers I'd driven up here with, I saw the same expressions of enjoyment and dedication as they'd always worn, whether competing or not. And I wanted it too – wherever I went. Contests or not, I could still love surfing on these shores.

This was going to work.

CHAPTER 2

A QUESTION OF FAITH: CROYDE BAY AND THE JESUS SURF CLASSIC

Surfing has always been regarded as spiritual to its faithful, so it's not really surprising that the organisation 'Christian Surfers UK' is such a huge movement within the sport.

Dubbed CSUK, the group have held an annual contest at Croyde since the beginning of time (almost) – and, oddly enough, the event has *never* been greeted by flat conditions. Rumours abound that they pray for surf, and it has a reputation for being a really fun event to be part of. This was just what I needed next, I thought – a no-drama, late-summer trip to North Devon with a bit of a contest thrown in as a side attraction.

It's not unusual for Britain to suffer immense droughts of surf in the height of summer. Even though my still-fragile love of my homeland was ever so slightly on the rekindle, I bailed to France for a couple of weeks in August – just to make sure the wave-count was nice and high before resuming this quest for a good surfing experience in the British Isles.

It was a wise decision. This year, as with most years, that sun-drenched flatness had run over from August into early September – when the Christians ran their contest. Naturally, all the relevant surf-predictor sites were still forecasting no surf at all by the time it turned up on the calendar, so a little faith was called for in deciding to go. If the Jesus Surf Classic was running then there would be surf, I reasoned. I was reminded of *Field of Dreams*, and the immortal line, 'If you build it, he will come.' It worked for Kevin Costner's character Ray, and so, I figured, it would for me.

Daylight hours had reluctantly started to shorten for the winter ahead, so it was already dark when I arrived in the little car park at Croyde Bay. I parked up, a few narrow lanes beyond the tiny crossroads of thick-stone pubs that did about ninety-nine per cent of their trade in two to three months of the year. The Ruda caravan park and campsite was tucked away behind me, sufficiently hidden from view by day so as not to interrupt the otherwise bare coastline and Clearwater Beach – which was actually owned by the same company as the campsite. I could hear the ocean only yards away, with its high tide lapping against the cooling sand, and decided to walk through the little lane that led to the almost empty beach. Was there any sign of the miracle swell these guys routinely conjured up?

Of course not. It was dead flat.

A figure was standing by the shoreline, alone, deep in thought. For a moment it made me nervous. Open-minded to the power of prayer, you could never rule out anything – especially when a sign over the marquee back on the beach mentioned 'walking on water'. In the darkness, the person in front of me could have easily been contemplating just that. I squinted and, as they came nearer, I recognised him as the director of CSUK, Phil Williams.

We knew each other quite well, because Christian Surfers ran a contest in my local beach, Rest Bay, every autumn called the Tsunami Cup. Due to my role as chairman of the Welsh Coast Surf Club, I'd been involved in helping them set it up as a fundraiser for Sri Lankan communities affected by the deadly Boxing Day tsunami.

Ironically, the Tsunami Cup had last year become one of my very few contest successes. Mind you, it felt odd winning in knee-high slop against a couple of juniors to claim an event that you helped found – kind of how the spoilt kid in the playground organises games so that he can beat everyone.

Still, it meant I knew a few of the CS guys, and I really liked the way they did things. They were exceptionally generous, benevolently minded people, and had never tried to force their beliefs on anyone. After years of waiting for the moment when their ulterior motives would finally reveal themselves, I had, like most other surfers, decided their kindness was genuine. Their desire to give to the sport of surfing was unconditional, and the worry they'd suddenly try to brainwash you had long been proved a false fear.

'How's things, Phil?' I asked, offering a hand.

'Not bad, boy,' he smiled back. 'Surf's a bit late getting here, but all's still going to plan.'

'Bit *late*?' I asked. 'Is there any coming at all?'

'Well, you never know. But we're going to keep praying.' He paused, as the two of us stared out at a two-inch, perfect, moonlit shore break. 'And I have faith.'

A few more conversational pleasantries were exchanged before I headed for the local campsite to find a place to pitch my new quick-assembly, pop-up tent (which I'd bought specifically for this ongoing re-discovery of British surfing). Meanwhile, Phil remained on the beach, coolly focused, hoping, waiting, praying.

Saturday morning emerged with soaking dew all around and a stiff, stiflingly cold offshore breeze. That faith Phil had mentioned was already being tested. Utter flatness – the kind that makes you abandon the beach for the day with no fear of missing anything – is what Christian Surfers were faced with.

And still they were not deterred in the slightest.

'Welcome to the fourteenth Jesus Surf Classic.' Phil's relaxed voice crackled out of the PA system that had been set up in the car park, just as I started to feel the first hints that today's sun might just carry with it a little bit of autumnal warmth. 'As you can see, conditions are not ideal yet, but we're registering people and will be returning at twelve to reassess the surf. Still hopeful that some heats can be run today.'

A couple of moans could be heard. Contestants began grumbling, some packing their bags for the journey home. To many of them Phil was a madman (albeit a friendly one), because Sunday's forecast was for conditions to be even smaller. Perhaps it came as no surprise to most, then, when twelve o'clock approached with no sign of any change in the surf predicament.

During this first wait I'd sat in the back seats of my friends' camper van, accepting their offer of repeated coffees and getting into the familiar routine of being at a contest that was 'on hold'. The Blythe family from Newport, about an hour up the motorway from Porthcawl, were regulars at UK surf competitions and always made the most of things. Their son, Rob, was on his way out of being a junior and competed in anything he could find – including contests on the continent. Anne was a school headmistress during the week and an ardent surf fan by weekend; while Bob divided his time between building houses and helping to run the administration of surf contests, including the Tsunami Cup. Bob was one of South Wales's true characters. On the way down to the Welsh one year I'd seen him at the side of the road, having run out of petrol. He claimed this was something 'every surfer in the world should try at least once'. Most of his stories from the sixties and seventies both began *and* ended in foreign jails and he was wildly opinionated on matters far and wide – from economics and politics to what odds Betfair should be giving on Cesc Fabregas scoring the first goal in the lunchtime kick-off.

When the midday call was for another two-hour adjournment, Bob naturally went straight to the bookies. Arsenal were playing Spurs this lunchtime – the former being my favourite team – although even that wouldn't tempt me to lose a tenner on some whimsical bet.

Still, as others upped and left, the chance to watch the match in the pub of the Ruda campsite kept me there – as well as a shaky belief that Phil and co were going to extract some surf out of the ocean by the end of the weekend, of course.

Many, many times have I ended up in pubs on the afternoon of a surf contest, watching either football or rugby matches. And, of those occasions, I'd say the reasons were split exactly fifty-fifty between drowning my sorrows over an early exit and whiling away time waiting for the next 'call' on whether to run some heats.

It's a stroke of genius by a good event organiser to postpone until just before kick-off for a big game. The lure of a quick pint (with plans for a coffee at half-time and then a drive home) often results in keeping annoyed competitors at the event. Naturally, it worked again here. A few of the Llantwit surfers had also turned up. As this was the next big surf town east of Porthcawl, there was always a heated rivalry between these guys and most of my mates, so any opportunity to wind each other up was taken with glee. On this occasion one of their ranks was an unlucky Spurs fan – and before long that quick pint had, even for those who'd been keenest to head home, was threatening to turn into several.

With a crew from Wales up for the night, I began mulling over my own options. It really did look as if there was no surf at all for days – and yet I had a feeling I should stay.

The best journeys allow important decisions to be made by circumstance, and this would be no different. Walking back to the beach, feeling pleased with myself for sticking to the one-drink-plus-coffee plan and enjoying the lukewarm sun on my back (which was no doubt enhanced by yet another victorious encounter for Arsenal), I bumped into Simon Tucker and his teenage son, Max. Simon was another Porthcawl surfer and a rep for Santa Cruz clothing. By mixing business with his trip down here, he'd been able to cover the cost of a bed and breakfast for the weekend.

'All right mate, how's things?' he asked, with a typically calm voice. The cadences of a man who had got used to waiting at surf contests – and indeed, beyond that, had got *good* at it. Temperament went a long way when events were 'on hold' – as the hapless Llantwit crew were currently proving with an impromptu afternoon on the piss.

'All right. Any sign of surf?'

'Nah,' he confirmed. 'Nothing. We'd stay, but there's this family thing tomorrow.'

Max looked up at him, forlorn. Simon continued.

'Max wants to hang around – the other groms are all still here – but he's got to be back too really. I mean, if there was even a tiny chance of surf we'd stay but, well, I checked Magic Seaweed again and it's impossible.' (Magic Seaweed is a well-known surf prediction site.)

'Fair enough,' I said. 'Not sure how sold I am myself on another night in a tent.'

That was when Simon came up with an idea: 'You can have our bed and breakfast room if you want. It's paid for.'

'Sorry?'

'Someone might as well stay there. You can get slaughtered with the Llantwit boys, then.' He put his hands over Max's ears.

'I had surfing in mind,' I replied.

Simon laughed. 'So did everyone else at nine o'clock this morning, mate. But I tell you, there's no way in hell there's gonna be even the slightest ripple.'

'Dad, you can't say "hell" here!' Max announced.

'Sorry, er, "heck"?'

'Same thing,' I frowned.

'Oh, whatever. It's all nonsense anyway – if it wasn't there'd be surf. So what d'you want to do? If you stay there I can give you the key now and you can bring our boards back for us – saves us going there again. Just tell the lady, Jenny, that you're me for tonight and she'll understand. We can shoot off straight away then.'

After thinking about it for a moment, I took the keys off him, bade them well and made for the car park to get the latest.

A pastor was running a skate competition on a temporary half-pipe, egging tiny kids to jump higher and higher off precarious pieces of coping, while others watched, soaking up the sun's high point – which out of the wind was amicably warm. Cake sales were raising more money for 'Surf Relief', the charity that CS supported at the Tsunami Cup, while beach volleyball volunteers, with cross-symbols on their T-shirts, gave out free lessons. A sign scrawled with a marker pen at contest control read:

Main event off until tomorrow – next call 8 a.m.
Paddle race at 4 p.m. – £5 entry – £70 first prize – see Phil for details.

Glad of having left the drinking to the others, I reached into my pocket to see if I had a fiver.

Oh well, I thought, looks as though I'm staying. There'd better be surf tomorrow.

That evening, over a couple of drinks in the popular surfers' watering hole, The Thatched Inn – a series of old, straw-roofed cottages just behind the main beach at Croyde – I took the chance to talk to one of the more prominent Welsh members of CSUK, Phil Johnson, about the definition of faith. He was known as 'Welsh Phil' – with the main man being 'English Phil' (even though his surname was Williams, which in my book made him part-Welsh anyway). Original nicknames, I know, but at least this way Welsh Phil and English Phil never got mixed up.

With all the stuff that had been written about Christianity lately – and books by Richard Dawkins and the like really attacking what these guys stood for – I wanted to know how they held onto their beliefs. I was also intrigued as to whether or not surfers were particularly open to the idea of faith. That said, after a day of flatness, which had for many turned into an afternoon of heavy boozing, there wasn't much of the spiritual on display around us right now. The night had yet again allowed temperatures to plummet, but inside The Thatch some live music and a swaying throng of worse-for-wear surfers was keeping things cosy.

'The most important thing about faith,' Welsh Phil explained to me, 'is that it *must* be tested.'

'What, like Job, you mean?'

'Yeah, I suppose.'

'Apart from the fact that Job is tested by Satan,' a friend of Phil's cut in.

'True.' Phil smiled. 'That's beside the point, though.'

'Go on,' I said.

'Well,' he explained, 'it doesn't work to try and bargain with God – like saying, "If you send swell, we'll believe in you." That sort of attitude will guarantee no waves. Get me?'

'Sort of.'

'You see, there may well be no surf tomorrow – and if that happens I'll accept that it's for a reason.' He paused to check I was still with him. I nodded to reassure. He continued. 'Prayer cannot be a simple list of requests that all get granted – otherwise a person's relationship with their Maker would be like a spoilt child to a bad parent.'

'I suppose. So is it everyone else's lack of faith that's keeping the surf away?'

I got the feeling Phil wanted to say yes, but his self-restraint was unbreakable.

'No. I don't know anything for sure, but I'm pretty sure of that one.' He leaned over to me, his voice a little lower. 'It's important to remember this,' he told me. 'God says no to some prayers for our own good.'

'I see. Well, what if I said I'd prayed for Arsenal to beat Spurs earlier?' I joked.

'You may well have,' Phil laughed. 'But it wouldn't have made the blindest bit of difference. I don't think the man upstairs interferes with things like that.'

'What, you mean sports?'

'Yeah.'

'But surf contests are sports.'

'I believe,' said Phil, deftly escaping my trap, 'that this year's conditions are a test of faith, and one we *will* pass. If, after we didn't get waves today, we still continue to believe that surf will come, then that's true faith.'

'And do you?'

'Do I what?'

'Believe there'll be waves tomorrow.'

'Absolutely.'

Although it may be an extreme example, Christians believe that a strong enough level of belief can move a mountain. It's a concept I've always admired, and one that has a huge relevance to surfing, and most other sports too. You can't doubt that belief is the most important prerequisite for surfing challenging waves like Teahupoo in Tahiti (also dubbed the 'End of the Road' because for some people it literally has been) or Hawaii's terrifying Banzai Pipeline, for example. The theory goes that if you believe in your imminent success in a pressurised situation, then you're halfway there. It's certainly true of my experiences in big surf – when you know you're going to make a wave, you do. But on the occasions when I've had an absolute pasting, I can always remember doubt sneaking in just before the moment of impact.

And Phil's lack of doubt was incredible to me. After a couple of beers I wandered back to the comfort of Simon's forsaken bed and started to entertain optimism. Maybe it would happen. After all, the only things forbidding it were the laws of oceanography. And what were they worth in the grand scheme of things? Maybe something had slipped past the wave buoys that forecasters, along with everyone else, had missed.

As long as we believed…

The following morning, as I should have foreseen, a mystery swell appeared on Croyde Bay's sandbars. I heard a few sceptics making their excuses as I walked to the beach to see for myself; several of them were scrambling to explain where these waves had come from.

'There was a blip forecast for an hour, like. It'll drop by the time they get a heat in the water.'

'Nah – September, man, long-range hurricane swells can creep in from the Caribbean. The Seaweed doesn't spot them.'

Surfers, for such a bunch of spiritualists, really don't like it when nature pulls off the unexplained. I wasn't objecting though – a day's surfing was on offer.

And an unorthodox one at that.

Annoyingly, once (English) Phil put a call out, it turned out there weren't enough competitors left in town to run the main, all-age-range 'open' category (which he decided to postpone until October). The other categories – which would always run first in smaller conditions anyway – were all present and accounted for, and by ten that morning the longboarders were taking to the water in disbelief. The draw for that one had a no-show in its midst, however, and there would be no question as to who was going to fill it.

Phil nodded his consent before I'd even asked. He instructed his wife, Annie, to move my open entry-fee over, securing me a spot in heat three. After borrowing a nine-foot noserider from one of the deputy beach marshals, it was time to take care of business.

The wind that had been pushing any swell back out to sea overnight had dropped, allowing the day to start warming up already. With it being low tide, I could see patches of wetter sand denoting where the sandbanks would be as the sea rose through the day. I suited up to the waist and walked towards the water's edge.

A series of peaks were breaking neatly across the beach at about knee- to waist-height. It would have been just a touch small for a shortboard but, with a nine-foot-six under my arm, the waves looked inviting. With no rips anywhere, the crisp lip-lines were peeling off symmetrically in both directions, thin curls of clear water cascading along the shoreline like dominoes.

As I arrived at the small group of altruistic volunteers and judges stationed at the water's edge someone took off on a set, arching his back and hitting a speed line right in the cusp of the breaking curl. As his longboard locked in, its momentum allowing balance where there shouldn't have been any, he tiptoed balletically to the nose, dipping one foot over the edge. Hanging five. This was surfing's weightless feeling, a miracle of gravity only possible for mere mortals on the most accommodating of waves. As the wave slowed, the rider fed his board back underneath himself before dropping a knee and hooking the craft back towards the fizzling white water – an even, crystalline wake of spray flowing from the tail as he went.

It was then that I realised the person riding wasn't a 'mere mortal'. It was Elliot – thankfully in a heat other than mine.

It wasn't long before my fellow competitors appeared – two of whom looked deadly serious, carrying lightweight, state-of-the-art boards festooned with sponsor stickers. As they stretched, and psyched, I pondered the paradox of approaching a sport as graceful and aesthetically inspiring as longboarding with such aggression.

'I'm keeping away from those two,' said my third opponent, as if reading my mind. Six-foot-tall, skinny and with a relaxed posture, he sat down on the warming sand and introduced himself. 'I'm Tim.'

This seemed more in keeping with the spirit of things.

'Tom,' I said, offering my hand.

'Hi Tom. I've never done a contest before. Don't get too offended if I ask you for a few tips as we go along?'

'Sure thing.'

A few minutes later Tim and I paddled out onto the left-hand side of the sandbar, putting us in just the right place to take turns on the right-handers – about as ineffective a strategy as could possibly be taken during fifteen minutes of 'competitive' surfing where the object is partly to steal waves rather than to share. But, given that longboarding was something I only really did back home on near-flat days when a shortboard wouldn't keep you afloat, I hadn't entered the category looking to do anything other than keep it light-hearted.

Although it may not be the kind of thing a surf coach would tell you to do, just having a surf without caring for anything else seemed to work wonders for my performance level. I picked off a couple of delicious waves – each of them with a wall running half the length of the beach towards Saunton Sands around the corner. Each time I paddled for another one I could feel this enormous, rising love for surfing coming from deep within me, a feeling I'd long forgotten.

Tim, meanwhile, was cruising across a couple of glassy faces himself, and it wasn't long before I noticed the beaming smile of someone who was having a surfing epiphany. As the ocean calmed for a few minutes, he started pouring his heart out. He worked in London as a barrister, had entered the contest because the whole idea of surfing and faith going together interested him and now, in the soul-lifting sunshine of this Devon morning, he'd realised, on the spot, that he didn't want to go back to his old life. It happens to thousands of people every year – but I'd never dreamed such a moment could occur *in a heat.*

But this wasn't any old heat. This was a heat that, by the laws of nature, shouldn't have been taking place.

As if enough divine intervention hadn't already been needed to get these waves here in the first place, a second stroke of fortune was befalling me. I'd taken no notice of the other two surfers, jostling away twenty yards to our north, which was just as well because they'd clumsily taken off on the same wave together in the dying moments of the heat. It meant one of them had incurred an 'interference'.

Interference is a dreaded term in a surf contest. Interfering with someone is every bit as dastardly as it sounds – and carries a suitably heavy penalty. It means taking off on someone else's wave – riding it when you've no right to and in so doing messing up the other person's scoring chances. It usually happens when people get over-competitive and jockey too hard for position in the line-up before the wave breaks. Thinking the other one hasn't caught the wave, the interferer then gets duped into riding a wave he or she shouldn't. The punishment is that you have part of your best wave score chalked off. As most heats are judged on your top two rides in the given time, this means you end up only being able to access a portion of the points available to your competitors, which can severely hinder your chances of progression to the next round.

What had happened between the two didn't concern me – or so I thought. As we all left the water Tim and I chatted, shook hands and promised to see each other around, while the sponsored pair were coming close to blows. The dispute was presumably over who had been at fault – who had interfered with whom, as it were.

The outcome of this little debate, I realised, affected me in the best way possible. The guy who'd interfered had lost an eight-point ride – relegating him into third place (an elimination spot) and allowing me through to the next round! By chatting and cruising with Tim I'd just advanced past a seeded longboarder. Perhaps I needed to take this approach in more contests.

Feeling rewarded for the faith I'd already shown, I tried to use the same doctrine of belief in my next heat a few hours later. As it happened, this second heat was slightly easier; the tougher seed having been (accidentally) dispatched in round one. Before I knew it, I was looking at a quarter-final berth. Someone was smiling down on me from above – it was the only explanation.

Meanwhile the swell had continued to build, now defying even Phil and Phil's expectations. By the time I'd arrived in the car park, the junior shortboarders were getting ready to go out into playful beach-break surf.

Reckoning I'd caught the belief that brought us the swell in the first place, it started occurring to me that perhaps the way to better my surfing did indeed lie in the spiritual.

Maybe I should say a prayer before paddling out or make the sign of a cross. That was maybe a step too far for me, so I opted to sit down in the sand before my next heat, regulating my breathing and trying to hone in on the mood of the sea.

It was now mid-afternoon during a hazy day of gorgeous, plump late summer. The sand had warmed, families were out playing on the beach and dogs were chasing balls or sticks, while their owners strolled barefoot in the encroaching shoreline.

And still the building tide pulled more swell in. This was like a surfing version of the feeding of the five thousand.

Alas the feeding of my longboarding ego was at an end. This third time around every other competitor was adept at cruising, carving, nose riding, lip bashing or whatever else the waves allowed. But with a bit more size starting to show, I had run out of ideas – finding the board hard to control in surf that would now accommodate a good session on a shortboard.

I convinced myself, however, that this was the consolation prize. With longboarding out of the way, and having already progressed more than I'd ever imagined, I came straight in to shore, grabbed my six-two from the car and ran back to the water without even considering waiting for the result. I was out of the running, and thrilled by the prospect. All that was left to do was surf the rest of the day away.

With plenty of room to the side of the contest area, this was a chance to revel in the reasons why Croyde Bay, on its day, is one of Britain's best beach breaks. Wedged into a little promontory between the vast stretches of sand that make up Saunton and Woolacombe, the place siphons off the best of any swell running. Waves then rise out of deeper water, hitting the beach with an unusual amount of power for this stretch of coast – meaning that on a clean swell the place can become a real barrel-fest, especially at low tide.

Closer to mid-tide now, the beach was just a constant series of clear-water, open-faced peaks, with sunlight glinting off them as they broke juicily towards an inside section that sped up before closing out yards from the sand. Given that the rest of the world had anticipated no surf this weekend, it was also unusually quiet for a Sunday afternoon in one of the country's most competitive breaks. Occasionally a youngster who had been knocked out would paddle over and vent his frustration by stealing a few, but it didn't bother me. I was full of surf stoke, and love for my fellow wave seeker.

Feeling the rays gently spreading warmth over the back of my wetsuit, I sat staring at my hand through the glassy water and waited for another set – when a voice called out to me.

It was Tim. He'd paddled up from the south end of the beach and I could see already he was still carrying the high from earlier.

'This is the life.' He smiled. 'I can't believe people do this all year long. I need to get myself down here as soon as possible!'

I nodded and then snagged another wave, weaving my way to the inside. Landing a little floater right on the shoreline, I turned to sprint-paddle back out for another one, energised and inspired by the ride I'd just had. I hoped I was one of the people Tim was talking about. I did spend most of my time living this lifestyle and right now the thought of feeling jaded or fed up with surfing – whether at home or not – was utterly alien to me. How had I ever allowed myself to get so ungrateful with my lot?

Whatever the answer, it wasn't going to happen again.

'We'd like to thank God, not only for sending his only son but for giving us surf in the end,' said English Phil at the presentation, as dusk set in around the car park and I towelled the life-affirming salt water of North Devon out of my hair. Watching from the open boot of my car, I spotted one of the two longboarders who'd argued in my and Tim's first-round heat making his way up to receive the second place trophy. The winner was a local lad – who'd seen off Elliot in a close final.

My wave-count for the weekend had been higher than I could have ever envisaged before driving up here on Friday night amid predictions of flatness – or even yesterday afternoon, as a pub full of surfers-turned-football-fans drank away their hopes of spending today in the water.

Some may call it stubbornness, I thought, and some faith. But ultimately the decision of CSUK to press on with this event against such odds was impressive. I tried to think whether I'd ever seen someone as convinced of the improbable as Welsh Phil had been last night. His outlook had surely caught on – and it felt as if the collective goodwill of everyone who'd made it to the beach today had conjured this swell out of the doldrums of summer flatness. Maybe you could be so in tune with the ocean that things would just happen for you like that. Some of the world's most famous surfers were reputed to be able to pull such tricks. I remembered stories of Tom Curren paddling up the beach at Huntington in the

US without reason, only to stroke into the wave of the day – not to mention his arrival at South Africa's Jeffrey's Bay back in the nineties for the ride that had inspired me to start travelling in search of waves.

Whatever you read into it, the outlook of the two Phils was something I reckoned all surfers could learn something from. Although what that something was I was still trying to figure out as I pulled in for petrol and prepared for the two-hour drive home to Wales – by which time nightfall would carry the earliest, chilly hints of the bitter months ahead.

There's something else that driving away from a session at night does to you. It allows the surf you've just had to slide back into your memory, and you usually rise the next day to the feeling it had all been part of some other life, some twist of fate that you barely deserved.

Was it any surprise, therefore, that when I made my way up to Porthcawl's seafront the following morning to check the surf that there wasn't a ripple in sight? Or that when I got back and went online to look at the swell readings every beach throughout England and Wales was flat? As I thought, less than twenty-four hours later, there was already the sense that perhaps this mystery swell *had* never existed. The late summer calm was back, as if to hush away any whispers of this preposterous, impromptu session.

Well, even if it had been, its effects were still with me. And I knew that autumn, with its almost infinite promise, was just around the corner.

CHAPTER 3
AN OVERNIGHT RUN ON BRITAIN'S BEST WAVE

Of all the seasons, autumn is surely the one that holds the most promise in the mind of a northern hemisphere surfer. It's the time of year when water temperatures remain high while the cooling land scares the tourists away – and sends the wind offshore, blowing out to sea and lifting the faces of oncoming waves, making them steeper and faster to surf. Wherever you are, it'll be the same. Swells start to get serious, building ominously and lasting for days at a time. The waning sun is something you forget about, just as your imagination postpones the tortures of the oncoming winter.

But once things turn, they really *turn*. There always seems to be a particular week of the year in which the remnants of summer seas in Porthcawl suddenly toughen into a frigid mass of winter briny. And in this particular year that week fell in early November. A series of days appeared so gloomy you hardly noticed it getting dark, along with the first flat spell since autumn.

Surfing drifted away into distant memory as the air developed a bite none of us had felt since the dying throes of last winter. I knew, with the first full frost of the year, that when a swell next appeared it would be time to don my thickest wetsuit along with gloves and boots, followed soon after by the dreaded neoprene cap.

So far I'd been getting it easy. My real test of faith would be in being able to maintain this stoke through the coming blizzards, gales, freezing fogs and deathly crisp dawn patrols. Reaching for the credit card and a stint on lastminute.com would be too easy an option – but a cop-out nonetheless.

Meanwhile, my girlfriend Breige (whose efforts to learn to surf I documented in *Riding the Magic Carpet*) had no need for such worries. In the seasons that had followed since *Magic Carpet* and my horrid experience of sitting in plaster and watching her surf perfect Costa Rican left-handers, she had become a respected surfer. So much so that she had just received an offer she couldn't refuse: an all-expenses-paid trip to Galicia as assistant coach for the Welsh Junior Team at the European Championships. Over a thousand miles south of Wales, the beach breaks of Ferrol in La Coruña would be a world removed from what was in store for Porthcawl in the immediate future. Then again, I supposed, if this was the worst form of jealousy I experienced as a boyfriend, I couldn't really complain.

'Enjoy it,' I said through gritted teeth. 'I'll have to try and rustle up a surf trip of my own while you're gone.'

The best way to deal with winter would be face on, I decided. And fortunately it wasn't long after Breige and the team's departure to northern Spain that my next opportunity arose.

Having decided running south would be the coward's option, as well as too much like imitating Breige, it was with instant delight that I received a phone call on the second Friday evening of the flat spell, just three days after she'd left. It was a close friend from Porthcawl, whom I'd recently alerted to my availability and willingness for wave-seeking in the British Isles. 'Rhino' was a renowned charger of heavy surf with a voracious appetite for thick reef breaks and foreboding weather charts, as well as someone I'd never seen be put off by a bit of cold, so I knew he was serious about this one.

'Tom. Rhino here. Me and Jeremy Evans are gonna go to Thurso. There's a mental swell showing on the charts and we've got room for one more. What you up to this weekend?'

'Nothing really. When you thinking of heading up?'

'That's the catch. How quickly can you be ready?'

'Pretty quick, like. When are you talking about?'

'How about ten minutes? Jem's with me now. We'll leave for yours right away if you're in. Have you got a gun, by the way?'

You may think this is an alarming thing to be asked before going on a surf trip to Scotland (home of the lauded reef break at Thurso East). And you'd be right. It's a downright terrifying thing to be asked to bring – but probably not for the reasons you're thinking.

A 'gun', as well as being a deadly weapon, is in fact the name given to a surfboard especially designed for catching and riding the biggest waves imaginable. Many people would probably rather be asked to bring the first kind with them, though, including me. If you need a gun of the surfboard variety, it means you're in for monster surf.

'I haven't got anything more than six-foot-three,' I replied nervously. 'Why? You expecting it big up there?'

Rhino chuckled and repeated my question quietly to Jem – who I promptly heard yelling something back.

'Will I need something longer?' I asked. (The bigger the wave, the longer the board – I only kept a six-three because I didn't often plan on riding anything that needed more length.)

'Yeah, you will,' Rhino replied, matter-of-factly. 'But it's OK. One of the boys in Thurso will lend you a gun. So, you in or not?'

'Er…'

'We need to know now, man.'

'OK. Yes. I am.'

And that was that. Ten minutes later we were fuelling Jem's van in the nearby Esso garage, with our next planned stop being Thurso in Caithness and the wave known among other things as Coldwater Nias – a reference to its uncanny resemblance to the world-class Indonesian point break of the same name, despite the fact the original Nias broke in front of tropical jungles and in an ocean warmer than a swimming pool.

Staring through the front window as the catseyes and white lines of the floodlit motorway disappeared hypnotically and endlessly beneath us, the thought that we were on our way to a surf session seemed out of kilter. Signs flew by for Stoke-on-Trent and Manchester, then Wigan, Preston, Carlisle – followed by the illegible Scottish names that show you're starting to get somewhere. Or so you think. In the case of Thurso, itself only a few miles shy of John O'Groats, you haven't really broken the back of the journey until Inverness is behind you.

I'd been to Thurso one time before – with Jem as it happened, on our way back from the Orkney Islands during the trip that later became part of *Riding the Magic Carpet*. At the time he went by the pseudonym of 'Joe'. His van had been our mode of transport then too and we'd been lucky enough to get the wave close to as good as it gets.

'This time we're gonna get it *absolutely* as good as it gets,' he grinned, allowing his eyes to drift away from the empty M6 for a brief moment.

There had been real method in the immediate nature of our departure. Jem, having worked for years as a rep in the north for the clothing company The Realm, knew exactly how to spot the right conditions for a solid Thurso swell and reckoned it was only possible to know for sure by checking the wind charts (usually on the BBC weather website) less than twenty-four hours before going. As it was a ten- to twelve-hour drive up there, this meant you needed to be on your guard and ready to drop everything.

'What's the time?' he asked Rhino, once we were several hours into the trip – and well on our way across England.

'Ten-ish.'

I could feel the van accelerating. 'So we've got nine hours till daylight,' Jem muttered aloud. 'We need to really cane it to catch the dawnie.'

A master at long journeys, he placed both hands on the wheel and straightened his spine as his right foot dropped again to add an extra ten miles an hour to our average speed. If he was right about the surf we could expect, then it would be worth any amount of time behind the wheel of a van.

With another cold, early winter night closing in outside, though, and only the monotony of the dark, straight lanes on offer as distraction, all three of us began to feel the need to sleep.

I was the first to nod off – pressing my face against the side window, leaning away from Rhino in the middle seat. Drifting in and out of varying levels of slumber, which is all you can manage in a barren Citroën Dispatch that's rattling its way along at ninety miles an hour, I began to lose track of the journey.

'Huh – check it out, there's a sign for Cumnock,' Jem laughed at one point. 'Imagine living there. You asleep, Rhino? Rhino?'

Rhino and Jem were one of the greatest buddy duos ever to surf around Porthcawl. Both were as dedicated to the lifestyle as you could get. Each worked in the surf industry, made a point of getting out on the road within Britain to score waves and had the same passion they'd probably enjoyed since first meeting each other as fourteen-year-olds. They both had a string of titles between them, including Rhino's modest haul of having been Welsh champion four times before moving away from the contest scene to have a family. Usually I wouldn't consider someone's contest CV as being important in introducing them to a story, but in Rhino's case it's important for you to know how gung-ho he could be as a surfer. With a build-up of speed and momentum that bordered on the reckless, he would absorb himself completely in the act – often looking as if he was waking from some sort of trance when he pulled off a wave having unwittingly demolished it. Jem, meanwhile, had garnered an equally fearsome reputation in big surf having spent months on end in Indonesia, where rumours were rife of his having played Russian roulette with all kinds of horrifying, life-and-death reef breaks.

And when the two of them got together the results could be carnage – especially with a swell on the go.

Given the fact I was bearing irreversibly towards a session in heavy surf with these two, it was understandable that sleep didn't stay with me for long. Rubbing my eyes, I soon sat up to look back around the cockpit of our van and realised one of us still hadn't logged a minute of shut-eye. Rhino had moved to the back and nodded off, leaving the same person behind the wheel since initial departure. Jem was a man possessed, staring ahead with tunnel vision. Better offer to take over, I thought.

'Want me to drive?'

'Nah, I'm all right for now,' he replied, showing determination in his now watery eyes. 'It's gonna be light soon, then I'll be fine.'

When light did start seeping out of the horizon, it began illuminating a frost-coated wilderness of flat grassland and plain rocky outcrops. This was the final run to the town of Thurso – at almost exactly the time Jem had predicted.

This is also the stage of a surf trip at which you get the most nervous. Until now you've been able to relax into a long journey, knowing that there's an almost infinite amount of time at your disposal to talk, wait, eat, sleep, change the CD, flick through a magazine, think about the surf ahead. With minutes to go before your first sight of surf though, you often start to get edgy. What will the waves be like? Will the wind be right? Once you realise that the time to sit and wait is almost over, anxiety takes control.

Until you get that first glimpse of the surf – after which worry usually dissipates and it's all about adrenaline. Usually.

Jem rolled his van smoothly and uneventfully through the yet-to-wake town centre of Thurso and on to a little farm track that led up to the point at the northernmost end. It rocked across the stony car park to the edge of a muddy verge – whereupon we were able to feast our eyes on a ten-wave set, each rising peak easily measuring triple-overhead in height. They were being groomed by an offshore wind, causing light wisps of spray to rise off as the waves barrelled wide and hard.

Neither of us said a word. The surf was enormous.

In front of the dilapidated castle that served as Thurso's second most important landmark (after the wave), we sat and stared. Surrounded by barns, a small row of houses and a few bails of hay, this little car park was deserted but for two vans and a car – each bearing surf stickers and empty but for the rolled up clothes that indicated exactly where you could find their owners. Grey skies dropped a light drizzle on us to usher in the new day, while the town remained still. Surfers here went about their business away from the eyes of most residents – the intensity of their experience, with its fear, nerves and ecstasy, was something to be endured discreetly, out of the way. If you got scared here, nobody would be around to sympathise. And if you wiped out the only people who noticed would be too busy trying to get a good wave themselves.

I remembered driving down this same little track years ago and recognised the cottage in which I'd been given a cup of tea by two of the top local surfers, Chris Noble and Scott Maine, after Jem and I had befriended them in the water. I knew that since then the Association of Surfing Professionals had run some big-money contests here (giving Chris, as a local, a wild card into a few that allowed him to surf against some of the best surfers on earth) – and that the wave had become a household name. Chris, who wasn't around this week, had warned me that if I ever came back I'd think things had changed but so far, early in the morning and in between a couple of storms, it looked as though Jem had helped us find a day that belonged to the Thurso of old.

We'd seen a very different side to this wave last time – on our way back from the Orkney Islands. It had been much smaller, tamer, user-friendly. 'Fun size', as most would call it. Then the emphasis had been on 'good'. This time it was huge, which may have been another reason for the apparent lack of bustling surfer activity. Out of the dark northern ocean, mountains of water were repeatedly rising and detonating before us.

Secretly, I was already hoping Jem might say something reassuring about how he too was a little afraid of what we had no choice but to do.

His first words, when he did break from the trance that had come with ending his marathon drive, were nothing of the sort:

'It's gonna be a job for the big boards. That's about as good as surf gets, man. Can you believe it? How good is that? How good? Let's do it!'

And with that he promptly peeled himself away from the driver's seat and stepped out, heading around to the rear of the van to suit up. In the blink of an eye he'd psyched himself up to it.

It was then I realised that Rhino was still asleep in the back. I wondered how many times in someone's life they would be able to awake and sit straight up to the sight of surf like this. If that were me, I'd need a strong coffee and a stretch before I could even think about heading out there.

But Rhino was just as keen. The opening of the back door was enough to stir him. He stepped out gingerly into fresh air, but his eyes were wide open within seconds. Guffawing, childlike, he jumped on the spot as the next ten-wave-plus set blasted across the flagstone reef. His moment of celebration was cut short only by his soaking wetsuit hitting him on the head. Jem was unloading all of our boards and gear, clearly intent on wasting no more time getting into the waves of his dreams.

His dreams.

I was scared. Neither of these two was going to have the slightest bit of time for that, though – as the sight of my own wetsuit flipping through the air towards me confirmed. It was followed by a banana.

'Some energy,' Jem grinned. 'You might need it.'

'Thanks,' I said, trying to look enthusiastic. 'Did you say something about being able to borrow a gun?'

'Oh yeah,' Jem paused for a second. 'Well, I've got a six-five. How's that?'

A surfboard six-foot-five in length would be painfully inadequate to negotiate drops the size of a small building.

But in the absence of a better offer, there wasn't a lot I could do about that. I'd have to just pick off the smaller waves and hope I didn't get ridiculed for it.

During the past fortnight winter had indeed been firming its icy grip. It was now late November, and we had gone and driven seven degrees further into the northern hemisphere – 600 miles closer to the frozen edge of the planet. Water is denser when cold – and the line-up here at Thurso East looked a dark, uninviting place. The black rocks below made the grey ocean surface appear dead calm, ruthless. Each time a wave broke in front of the ledge that defined the take-off spot, it would make a tremendous crashing sound. From the comfort of the car park, the thick, perfectly turning tubes were a thing of awe and beauty. But from the channel, halfway towards paddling out, it was like staring into the eye of some undiscovered, misunderstood monster.

It had been well over a week since I'd last surfed, so my wetsuit had been dry at least. While that made getting ready a slightly warmer affair than for Jem and Rhino (who kept theirs in buckets rather than airing them anyway), it had led to feeling a bit out of tune and rather rusty. As if I may need a few waves to get back into the swing of things. Again, this was a luxury I'd have to forego. It was do or die out there – which was just the way my two travel companions liked it.

Jem had led proceedings so far and this was also to be the case in the water. The man who had driven us up here overnight, without resting beyond stopping for petrol, timed his arrival into the line-up just right. Each of the other surfers had just ridden a wave, allowing him to be in place to set himself up for a huge peak, unchallenged apart from the encouraging hoots from me and Rhino. With a look of calm concentration he took a deep breath, summoned up the energy needed, aimed for Lord Thurso's castle back on the shore and began paddling. I saw his eyes widen as he pushed himself over a ledge, before the tremendous pull of water towards the trough of the wave caused me to pull back from watching any further. A squall of spray lifted off the pitching lip, dousing us in sea water as an explosion of white water went up. And that was the last of Jem – until he popped up casually, still standing, into the channel at the end of what must have been a spectacular first ride.

Rhino yelled his approval, as I noticed two of the other surfers who had been in place to see the whole of Jem's wave congratulating him. Jem had a wild grin emblazoned on his face and was practically drooling as he made his way, as fast as he could, back to get another one.

'Reckon he got barrelled then?' I asked Rhino. Getting 'barrelled' was just about the greatest sensation in surfing – meaning to place yourself inside the tube of the breaking wave with enough forward momentum to shoot along with it.

Rhino's face foretold the answer: 'I *know* he got barrelled then.'

A brief lull in sets followed, allowing all the other surfers to gather in the line-up again – including Jem, who was only too eager to confirm the quality of the wave he'd just had.

'The hole at the end of that thing was miles in front of me then,' he boasted – explaining how deep behind the curl he had gotten. 'That was mental!'

When another row of waves appeared, Rhino was naturally next in line.

This time I didn't make any effort to watch him – opting to concentrate on my own positioning instead and paddling safely over the wave. This would leave me ready to try and pick off one of the next ones. Jem had made getting into one of these look so easy and I knew my best bet of making a real go of this was to get stuck in from the off.

The problem facing me now was that a few of the other surfers had themselves got into a better place than me. In surfing there exists a common rule that the person sitting closest to where a wave begins breaking has the right to take off – and a guy on a big red board had made his way right to the top of the peak. This meant I had to let him go, and make do with the third wave of the set.

Checking that the wave had lined up properly, and wasn't going to shut down on me after I got in to it, I began paddling. Trying to ignore that I was on a board far too small, I kicked frantically with my feet and prepared for the final push. I felt the wave pick me up as I grabbed the edges of my board. My stomach suddenly felt as if it had done a somersault as I saw the drop below me open out. Gasping with trepidation, I threw all my weight to the back of the board, making the bottom half of my body act like an anchor, saving myself from dropping in. The wall of spray blinded me as the wave leaped forward, unridden. Shame began to absorb me immediately. You only get a few chances at taking off in a place like this before the other surfers decide you don't mean business and stop giving you the opportunity to paddle for the good ones. I knew without a doubt I'd just blown the first of those few chances.

A series of even bigger waves behind that sent everyone scrambling in different directions. Apart from Jem, who swung midway up the face of the next one and swooped downwards, sliding into the tube at the same time as getting to his feet. To make things harder, Jem was surfing with his back to the wave, adeptly grabbing the side of his board (known as the rail) for stability as the ice-like curtain slid over him. This was world-class surfing. In these intense conditions, Jem had wasted no time in raising his game to meet the challenge.

Fortunately, all of this meant he probably hadn't noticed me baulking at the one before.

I sat up for a moment as the waves again let off. I tried to remember other times I'd surfed enormous waves – as well as the perfect and ferocious tubes I'd seen at this very spot all those years ago. It was the size of this swell, and comparative winter-like nature of the scene around, that was taking so much adjusting to. Focussing on my breathing, I recalled the most important tip anyone had ever given me about this kind of surf: paddle for a wave as you normally would – but then add an extra stroke with each arm before jumping up. This would allow for the additional speed with which a wave like this would pitch forward as it broke.

Drawing my best attempt at quiet confidence, I locked a wave in my sights and began the splashing sprint towards the ledge, and glory. A lurching, heaving, guillotine of water launched itself at the reef in front of me, as I swallowed my fears and lowered my feet towards the board that was now dropping away from me, down towards the pit. Again I felt that stomach-churning warning signal within – but this time I managed to override it, and felt the resultant adrenaline flood my veins as I reached the bottom of the wave intact. Survival instincts now running on a state of heightened awareness, I drove a bottom turn and tried to find a good point in the middle of the face to generate the speed needed to get safely to the end of the thumping section. Trimming mid-face, I felt the acoustics around me change. The water in front darkened as the roof of the wave hovered just behind my head, interrupting the sounds of the outside world. I could feel a vacuum of air around as the tube breathed somewhere very close, before the pressure eased and I accelerated for the flatter shoulder of the wave. Confidence immediately boosted, I jammed a cutback in, as if to stamp the ride, and pulled off feeling pretty pleased with myself.

'Not bad,' Jem grinned as I joined him on the paddle back out. 'You've got to slow yourself enough to be in that tube next time though. No point throwing yourself onto a rail all cocky like that if you haven't pulled in first.'

By 'on rail' he meant carving a turn – because that would involve turning your board onto its 'rail'. And by 'pulling in' he meant turning into the tube of the wave. In Jem's world a big carve was meaningless here without a tube ride to precede it, and that was easier said than done.

I told him I'd heard the tube behind me and that it couldn't have been far off, to which he replied by asking, 'Did you see the hole?'

'You what?'

'Simple question. Did you see the hole? If you did, it was a tube. If you didn't, then it's back to the drawing board. It's all about barrels here. That's the only thing you should care about.'

As we were talking, Rhino dropped into a mid-sizer right in front of us, ramming all his weight onto the tail as he reached the bottom, killing off his speed and allowing the wave to overtake him. Setting his line through the middle of the tube, I noticed his right hand dragging softly against the face as he raced past us. This was his way of controlling speed inside the heart of the wave.

'Now *he* would have just seen the hole,' Jem explained. 'Just in case you're wondering, *that's* how it's done.'

Merely watching that wave had sent my heart rate through the roof – and all I wanted in the world was to get into that position myself, whatever it took.

It's easy to think such things paddling out, though. When you're actually poised to drop into a wave like that, a lot more is going on to put you off. The window of time in which to act is so limited that fear freezes you to the spot.

Getting into a session like this for most surfers, myself included, is a battle against your better instincts, as you dare yourself to catch the wave later and later, each time making the ledge in front of you get that little bit closer to being completely vertical.

The other thing running through my mind at all times was the fact that the two guys I'd driven up with were from the same town as me, and that whatever happened up here would get back to everyone I knew and had grown up with. Usually when you came across waves of such quality it would be abroad, with hardly anyone you knew – and in a competitive line-up of surfers hungry for waves, who didn't give a shit if you'd just had the wave of your life. Such an atmosphere could be as cold as any of the weather-engineered situations you'd find up on this very north-eastern tip of the British mainland. But this time the only thing frosty about the atmosphere was in the literal sense. The surfers I was sharing this session with would do nothing but encourage me to score the wave of my life.

After about five attempts to get in and around the tube, one virtually landed on my lap. As if meant for me, everything suddenly slipped into place and all semblances of things being hard, difficult, tricky or frightening took ten seconds' leave. Just enough to allow me a ride that would stay with me forever.

A peak so round and solid that you wanted to cry with excitement made its way through the ocean towards me, just as a burst of rain began to pour out of the light-grey skies. Apart from where the droplets broke its surface, the water appeared silvery, slippery, thick. There wasn't a wisp of wind and I was in exactly the right position to go for it, with no hassle from anyone else.

I paddled, coolly focussing my breathing and senses to channel the excitement in my muscles into the economy of motion needed to negotiate the drop. Building up paddle momentum I got over the ledge well in time to avoid any kind of freefall, but still deep enough along the reef to find a long wall of mercury-like water rising up in front of me. Way beyond, out in the flats and a world I had left behind, I could see Rhino sitting up and raising his hands into the sky. He was yelling something. Time began slowing and my awareness of all around me heightened to a haywire crescendo. I could hear my breathing as my thought processes clarified... *This wave is going to do it... It's going to do it... It's going to...*

The lip hooked itself outwards, piercing the flat water to my left, swallowing me in the back of its saltwater pocket. With so much room, my board was able to stick to a clean wave face and continue unhindered in its trajectory forward, towards the window of light that had now shrunk my view of the channel to merely a snapshot – with Rhino cheering ecstatically in the middle of it. This time the absolute change of sound, gravity and atmosphere indicated how far behind the portal I was. There was time to think, to stare, to marvel – then as quickly and predictably as it had thrown over, the exit suddenly flew towards me and I was catapulted out and back into reality, careering onto the shoulder with runaway speed and a grin that could be seen from the town centre.

Taking a breather to register what had happened, I let the euphoria flood through me and waited for my psyche to adjust. I had to try and do it again.

Paddling back out to wait my turn again, I watched as Jem slouched his way through another delirious chamber of churning water.

A couple of the other surfers took off on the waves behind, including one who got hung horribly in the lip as it rose up. Kicking his board away he was hurled through the air and downwards to the waiting reef, as a choir of groans and cheers echoed through the channel. The exploding white water released him to the surface, and a hero's reception. He'd need a trip to the car park though, as his board had not survived the thrashing intact. I watched as he gathered his senses and then noticed that only the half attached to him by a cord had survived. He gave a knowing look – a look of resignation and mild satisfaction – even pride. It had obviously happened to him many times before.

Several exchanges of waves followed – allowing both Jem and Rhino to continue registering oodles of tube time – before I again found myself in position for another monster wave. This time I relied less on instinct and more on the memory of how I'd ridden the one before.

Again, the wave allowed me to get down it with all my speed and poise intact, and I turned to take aim, watching with relish as the shoulder thickened. A darkening pit began to rise around me. I knew what to do here, I thought, seizing my chance to repeat things. But this time I'd do it with a casual stance I'd not dared to pull before.

As I heard the other two cheering for me, I clasped my hands behind my back and stuck out my tongue. The tube held up for me, and for a moment I was able to feel myself standing disdainfully inside one of the heaviest tubes I'd ever seen, as bona fide witnesses from Porthcawl, my *home town*, hollered at me.

Things can happen awfully quickly with so many thousands of tons of water flying about the place – and just before making my cocky escape and reaping the imminent glory, I saw Jem's expression change ever so slightly. His eyes had widened, almost unnoticeably, but enough to warn me that something wasn't quite right. The next thing I felt was an enormous whack to the back of the head, before I flew backwards and was pummelled downwards into the reef, cracking off the floor, coccyx first. The panic that set in began to drain me of oxygen, and it was with a splutter and whimper that I pulled my head above the surface – just in time to have to dive under the wave behind.

The violence of all that water exploding on the reef shuddered through my body, yanking my limbs in different directions, shaking me until I didn't know which way was up. I could feel cold water pouring in through the back of my wetsuit as the wave ripped a piece of Velcro open. The shock gave me a surge of determination to get back on my board and paddle my way to safety.

Although the whole thing had taken seconds, it felt as if I'd just survived days at sea when I broke free of the impact zone and dragged myself towards the safety of deep water, wondering what had just happened. Jem was shaking his head and tutting.

'Pride comes before a fall, young man!'

Rhino laughed.

'I could see that lip creeping towards the back of your head then,' Jem added. 'Made that mistake myself once. You shouldn't assume you can squat in a tube like that unless it's the size of a truck. You end up forgetting where the lip is. That, fair play, was the funniest thing I've ever seen – one second you were about to fly out of the barrel of your life and the next you looked like a rag doll!'

'Oh, come on,' I pleaded. 'It was a good one before that happened!'

'Nope,' Jem grinned back, shaking his head. 'That's the whole point of tube riding. It's the risk. The more you stake, the more the reward. If you fall you only get about a tenth of the credit. It's back to square one for you. You'll just have to do it again now.'

'Whatever,' I spat back and looked to Rhino for some sort of support.

'Rhines'll tell you. That's the way it is,' Jem added, as if he'd read my thoughts.

Rhino didn't have time to reply, fortunately perhaps, having spotted an incoming set and heading off in pursuit of it.

As we settled in to a marathon session, I started realising that things wouldn't automatically keep going my way. When we'd been in half an hour I noticed that on rare intervals there were sets coming through way bigger than any others. The trouble now was that this interval had begun shortening. At first it was every quarter of an hour, but then it dropped to ten minutes. It was clear the swell was growing – and fast.

If my board had carried unfortunate dimensions at the start, it was now rendering surfing virtually impossible. Getting down the earlier waves had been possible with a gargantuan paddle effort and a reliance on not a drop of water being out of place. Now though, with a wind starting to build alongside the swell and limbs rapidly reaching the point of extreme fatigue, staying out much longer could be perilous – and anything but fun.

To my dismay, Rhino had a solution:

'My six-ten is getting a bit small for this now,' he stated, matter-of-factly. 'I might go in and get the seven-o. Want to take this one off me if I do?' He pointed at the board he was paddling. 'Anything's gonna be better than that thing you're on!'

'Yeah. For sure.' The offer of an extra five inches of stability and foil would decrease my chances of further injuring my already sore coccyx – although only marginally.

The spectacular part of his plan involved swapping boards on the spot, while treading water. Nervous a set might catch us catastrophically unawares, I ripped my leash off quickly and concentrated on securing this new ride to my right ankle.

Next came the bit I most wanted to see. Spitefully, I was wishing for a case of *Schadenfreude*; secretly hoping he'd get creamed catching one in on my board – and then exalt me for having managed to get this far on such an impotent piece of equipment.

With a kick of water he dug in to a paddle, making for another enormous wave. After chasing it to the very top of the reef, he spun around, drifting halfway up the face backwards. With a couple of quick strokes at the critical moment he engaged with the wave's forward momentum, allowing his own weight to launch him into an air-drop – only inches ahead of the tumbling lip.

My six-five looked like a skateboard under his feet as he landed, lodging just enough of the tail into the water to skip up the face again before the curtain landed behind him.

Far from safe yet, I saw him adjust his weight to try and compensate for the over-responsiveness of the tiny board he was riding. Flexing under the pressure and speed, my six-five wobbled as a puff of gas billowed from the depth of the furious tube, lifting Rhino's wet hair as if he were standing in a wind tunnel. It was a show of skill and bravado that I couldn't even imagine attempting myself.

Jem hooted. '*Yeeaah buddy!*'

'Did he make it?' I called over.

Jem laughed. 'No. Don't be daft! He just got annihilated. Good effort though, eh? You can rely on the Rhines to go when no one else would!'

It was at that point that I remembered Jem hadn't slept yet since driving up. By highlighting Rhino's approach, he was taking attention away from his own relentless display of commitment.

'Are you feeling it yet?' I asked.

'Not in any way whatsoever!' he replied. 'Leap before you look, innit!'

As it happened, the fierce peak Rhino dropped into was one of the last to barrel like that. Scotland has always lived at the mercy of whatever weather systems the ocean chooses to generate, and the same storm that had sent these waves was itself beginning to make its way to shore. Jem had predicted this as early as yesterday – which was why he had been able to plough his all into this session, with no need to keep anything in reserve.

After nearly five hours of surfing, it was clear the building breeze had ruined the waves. Gone were the airbrushed borders of the lip line, and the cylindrical tubes with their hypnotic, churning foam patterns. Instead the waves were crumbling, bouncing – their strict lines getting interrupted by a backing wind. But by now it didn't bother us in the slightest, and it was with serene relief that I climbed back on to the beach and up to the van.

For me, this was the point at which I could really begin to enjoy the stoke of a surfing experience as intense and fulfilling as any I'd known – on or off this little group of islands I called home.

Drained of the ability to do much more than hold his head up, his voice husky, eyes reddening and glazed – Jem drove us a few hundred yards back in to town, where we pulled up at a Tesco.

'I'm too tired to eat – but I need to or otherwise I'll never wake up again,' he mumbled, walking in a daze towards the fruit section.

Ten minutes later, he was snoring upright in the driver's seat of his van. After driving all night, and surfing for five hours in surf of such force many people would have been worn out within one, we figured he deserved the chance to recharge a little.

'We should offer to do some of the driving on the way back,' Rhino suggested, discreetly closing the door. 'But I reckon we leave him for now. Fancy a walk to the seafront?'

It was about a mile back to a point from which we could watch the North Atlantic, now unrecognisable, ushering in the rising storm. Grey skies were giving way to patches of darker cloud as we crossed the main river on a bridge. Below us brown, peat-tinted water rolled towards the sea from a river current. Between bouts of drizzle, the town still appeared to have barely come to life, as we passed empty pubs and hotels. A neat grid of streets hid behind a low-key seafront. Gloomy and under-populated, I noticed most of the shops were closed – apart from a chippy in which two teenagers waited, gazing at the floor, for their food to be cooked. A car pulled up to a crossroads, where a red light held it for far too long, with no other movement in sight – and still the driver waited, unquestioning. It looked as if the place lived on permanent call for a tourist season that I imagined to be brief and frustratingly fickle. With one of the moodiest patches of ocean on the planet just offshore, this would forever be a sea-battered, beleaguered town – clinging to the edge of an energy most of its inhabitants could barely understand.

We'd taken some snacks with us and sat down to eat. From a sea wall we were able to look over at the great, rolling mountains of white water that had overrun the line-up in which we had, only an hour before, been harvesting waves it may take us years to find again.

There was little sign now that the patch of reef in front of that timeless castle could host such a display. No evidence that surfers the world over stared at images of its almost mythical perfection.

As a gust lifted my hood from my forehead, my mind was taken back to that one wave – that almost-ride.

'Rhino?' I asked. 'How close was I to making that one – you know, the wave that clipped me?'

He paused.

'I mean, if I'd ducked just a little…' I began.

With a mouthful of Mars bar, he raised his hand. I stopped.

'Don't worry about that,' he said. 'Inches or metres, it's all the same. You didn't make it, and that's that. Better you go home with something to regret, anyway. If you'd had a perfect session then it'd be time to quit. This way, you've got something to make up for next time you catch a wave like that. Coz there will be a next time. You know that, don't you?'

I nodded.

And then I wondered what chance there was of that being on British shores. Yet again, like Jem's staring in at me from that shoulder, my eyes had opened that little wider. I'd caught the best tube of my life – almost. In Britain. Almost.

CHAPTER 4

LOSING TO AN INVISIBLE LONGBOARDER: THE GREAT NEWGALE RIP-OFF

Many, many weird and wonderful things can happen at surf contests around the UK – after all, it takes a screw loose to want to attend the things in the first place. Most are run in conditions ranging from the sub-standard to the utterly dire, during freezing weekends in places that take an age to get to, while all the rest of your mates are at home, warm and entertained.

And yet people still lap them up, including me. I've wasted hundreds of hours shivering in car parks, waiting for an announcer to confirm that my reason for being there was, well, not good enough – and yet for some reason I'm still drawn to competitive surfing. Some people don't even think the act of wave riding can become a competition, but I've always enjoyed the challenge of trying to convert rides into points and line-ups into game plans. Perhaps it adds a dimension to the otherwise highly frustrating life of a British surfer – if the act itself of riding the pitiful waves isn't that riveting, then solving the conundrum of how best to string a heat together can hold some reward in its place.

Something else I have to admit to liking about contests, though, is the sheer farcicality of some of the situations you see. As I said, something needs to be slightly amiss for you to want to go to them in Britain, and when a large group of similarly minded people – who are all missing some aspects of sanity themselves – get together in the cold to grumble over dreadful waves, there usually comes a point when you realise it's actually a cracking laugh. Until you lose, of course.

However, I do fondly remember one contest in which even losing was funny – because it was to a surfer who didn't seem to exist, in a contest so supremely weird in organisation and purpose that it stands forever in my mind as one of the best I've ever been to. It was such a great event that it didn't even have a name.

When rumours of this speciality surf-off first started, it was under the name-tag 'South West Student Championships' – which was in fact pure plagiarism. I later learned that the real South West Champs, run with clockwork efficiency by some huge sporting governing body, had taken a two-year hiatus due to lack of funding – allowing a hotelier in northern Pembroke to run a pretend version of his own. What could go wrong?

A lot, of course, but this didn't seem to trouble the bold entrepreneur one bit, as by the time people realised they'd entered a joke contest he'd already sold them a hotel bed and too much alcohol to be able to drive home. It was a genius business plan. *Dragons' Den* would have backed him in an instant.

I should have known something was fishy about the whole deal when I asked him on the phone about entering. You needed to be a student to get in, which was fine because I was in my third year at Glamorgan Uni at the time, but still the lack of rigour shown in vetting my entry was the first hint that his contest organisation may turn out to be a little, er, laissez-faire…

'Oh, we loosely say "students",' the middle-aged organiser, Terry, explained, 'but a few locals sometimes fill the draw if it's needed. Ones who go to college up here, see.'

He meant Haverfordwest, and the contest was being run at Newgale – which is, without exception, the worst beach break in Wales that anyone is yet stupid enough to try and surf. But bad beach breaks are a prerequisite for Welsh-based surf contests, so nobody was going to bemoan that at this early stage. (You leave that gripe until the mid-point of your round one heat – when you can do nothing about it other than surf very poorly and blame the conditions.)

'Yes, we run a relaxed event, you know. It's just a chance for some people to come and stay here off-season for a cheaper price and have a good shindig. I reduce the beer too – since you are all students. And then there's a surfing championship on the side.'

'I see,' I said. By 'reduce the beer' did he mean lower its price tag, or was he talking about some horrid distilling process that made the stuff worth less anyway?

'Yes, yes, you'll like it up here,' Terry continued. 'We always like to reward something different in the surfing. Judges can be a bit, you know, *boring* sometimes, I think.' Finally, here was a sentiment that I could relate to.

'Cool. Sounds good.' I said.

'Yes, you should have seen last year's final. The chap who won – local lad he was… Well, he rode off the back of one wave and then, before he'd got off his board again, the one behind picked him up and he carried on and rode that one in to the beach instead!'

At this point the thought crossed my mind that Terry might not know a lot about the conventional judging criteria of a surf contest, but I refrained from interrupting.

'I mean, you had to be there to believe it. It really was *spectacular*. Stood out to me by a mile, you know. So I said to the judges that they needed to make him the winner, and everyone was very happy with the outcome. It's nice for a new face to win something.'

As someone who mounted the podium all too rarely, this was music to my ears, and I resolved to ready myself to try 'spectacular' pull-outs – whatever they might be – at the first opportunity. I had just got some insider information on what the judges were looking for, and was going to make a good go of becoming the 'new face to win' this time around.

When you study English Lit and Media at uni the lecture timetable can often be a little light – which is great for surfing. However, luck would have it that the Friday afternoon before the South West Student Championships coincided with one of the few lectures that I could not miss at any cost, as I planned to write an essay on its subject material. This meant there was no chance of making it up to Nolton Haven – where the event's on-site accommodation was situated – until after dark. Not only did this prevent a practice surf on the eve of my round one heat, but it also allowed the full force of a bitter winter frost to set in before I got there.

Shivering in the dark, I set about finding two friends who had agreed to attend the contest with me – a pair of Irish brothers called Andrew and Al, who were always game for a surf-off – as well as working out where exactly I was going to sleep.

Andrew and Al lived in Plymouth at the time, where they were both studying. Although surfing was usually an individual sport, some events did keep a tally of 'team' points – like the way an athletics meeting will log medal numbers. This was going to be the case here, although it wouldn't mean anything to me as nobody else from Glamorgan Uni, to my knowledge, did contests.

That was far from the case in Plymouth, where Andrew and Al enjoyed being the best of a deep field of surf enthusiasts. They were both of them pretty humble about it, and took the lifestyle very seriously, letting their antics on a wave do the talking – rather than getting sucked in to the other popular habit of the student surfer: telling tall tales to members of the opposite sex. Their car was parked at the side of the road, so I pulled in behind it.

Terry had promised to put us all up for a tenner each, which sounded great. However, we had failed to anticipate the fact that this tenner would see us all shivering to sleep in one double room, curled into foetal positions in all our clothes. It was out of season and therefore the heating had been switched off. The sight of your own breath blowing steam into a room bathed in moonlight due to the lack of curtains is never conducive to a good night's sleep.

'You should have come down to the pub and had a drink with everyone else!' Terry berated us the next morning, when Al told him how we'd all developed backache in the overnight freeze. 'That's what everyone else does. You have no problem sleeping if you take proper advantage of a pound a pint.'

'But we kind of wanted to surf well today,' Al explained.

The hotel Terry ran, although right on the coast, was a ten-minute drive south from the beach where the event was being held. Arriving by night we'd seen little of the drive across Pembroke, but this early morning run along a winding ocean-side road to the car park that would become contest control was a chance to see the clear, cold and powerful Atlantic, grey and plumped with swell. As we left the little village we'd stayed in behind, heading north for Newgale's beach, trees and buildings seemed to back off. A basic landscape of light green fields was all the regular and relentless sea wind allowed, along with a handful of smaller stone buildings, most of which were boarded-up booths intended to serve the summer influx, and an almost deserted track. Its discreet humility allowed us to feel the dominating presence of the sea, as well as helping us to forget our uncomfortable night. The idea of a drunken rabble of students descending on this quiet place jarred with me.

Terry brought us back to reality, though, with a nonchalance that meant we were starting to feel like the outcasts for turning up rested and sober – as if by behaving like athletes we'd in some way dishonoured the event.

'Yes, do it your way, but don't forget the spirit of things!' said Terry, as he wandered off towards the motley bunch of contest officials he'd assembled. His two judges looked more like over-worked farmhands than experts in the art of surfing. One was haggard and lanky, with fingerless gloves and rotting teeth, which he surely wasn't helping by chain-smoking throughout the morning. The other was a little more physically healthy in appearance, with a shaved head, stocky frame and small eyes (which were exceptionally close together) in a chubby, freckled face. From the way he nodded at everything the other said, he didn't seem to be very keen to think for himself. The third judge did not exist.

Already this is a huge problem for a surf contest. Three judges are needed as a minimum or you risk either having split decisions or identical wave-scoring when they confer. Ideally there should be enough to have three on the panel for all heats, while others rest and a head judge oversees the whole thing to make sure that the scale is appropriately met.

Terry claimed to be that head judge, although as he was also doubling as beach marshal, runner, tabulator and scribe – not to mention contest director, hotelier *and* pub landlord – it was clearly not a role he was going to be able to perform to maximum effect, even if he'd known anything about the criteria.

As if these carefully chosen officials weren't already making this contest something of a lottery, the waves also posed a significant challenge. Having warmed up a little in the car, I stepped out into the wall of freezing air and walked towards the edge of a barren and almost infinitely long pebble beach to assess what I would shortly be paddling into.

February is probably the most excruciatingly cold month of a surfer's winter, and the dreaded phenomenon of the 'ice cream headache' was ever present. If you dipped your head below the surface more than twice in a few moments, even with a wetsuit hood on, your head would seize as if in a vice. The ice cream headache is instant and excruciating, running around your temples and forehead as all the blood vessels spontaneously constrict in reaction to a sudden change in water temperature. Because of this you don't want to have to duck-dive a lot in winter surf.

You needed to duck-dive a lot in this surf, though.

The merciless sea at Newgale Beach had thrown up a solid swell, breaking a long way out to sea. Normally such clean lines, stacked way out to sea and groomed neatly by a frigid offshore breeze, would be a welcome sight to good surfers, who'd see the waves on offer as being worth the paddle and head pain. In clean conditions you'd often be able to slip around waves on your way out too, rather than having to duck-dive every set. Not here, though. Any hope of reaching the line-up without your head almost dropping off faded at the sight of uniform close-outs.

A uniform close-out is a wave that closes out, or shuts down, with such blanket totality that there is not one point along the entire beach at which a surfer could ride across it for even a nanosecond. This is what Newgale was doing that morning. Sorry – this is what Newgale does *every day of every year since the dawn of time.* Or every single time I ever go there, at the very least. And it's a long beach too; well over a mile, so that's a hell of a close-out.

Slipping into freezing wetsuits, we contemplated the sight of these waves, shutting down and exploding like an Old Spice advert, blowing trapped air out of the back as thousands of tons of cold ocean folded in on itself. A few miles in either direction we knew there were probably surf spots firing, while we set about the task of negotiating a heat of hung-over beginners in thundering close-outs. There was probably more chance of needing to resuscitate your opponent on the wet sand than getting a decent opportunity to prove your surfing ability over him.

Fortunately, Andrew, Al and I survived round one with little more than bodies frozen to the core. All three of us had formed identical heat strategies: take the smallest wave, drop straight down it as early as possible and then try gliding across the already broken white water for our only manoeuvre. The bigger sets would break too powerfully to allow you any chance of getting back up the wave after dropping in, so this would only work on the tiniest ones – otherwise the bounce of foam would just smash you, offering no reward other than another horrid paddle.

Even this plan of attack was not effective enough for some of the more serious competitors – and by eleven that morning we'd seen a very accomplished surfer from Plymouth, who both Al and I had considered one of the event favourites, lose to someone who looked as if they could barely swim. He'd spent far too long fighting to get out the back, only to pick waves that threw him straight off. Meanwhile, to the jubilant applause of a group of mates, beer cans in hand, an unknown on an eight-foot mini-mal (a round-nosed board often used to give extra balance, at the expense of manoeuvrability) had waded out to waist deep and proceeded to catch a series of already broken waves that he rode straight to the beach, tentatively squatting for fifteen seconds a time. In theory any surfer who catches an unbroken wave out the back should, just because of the degree of difficulty involved, be rewarded with a much higher score than someone employing this inferior approach, which was basically that of a complete beginner. But throwing in a healthy dose of appalling judging, miracles were likely to happen. It meant we would have to treat a surfer of any ability as a serious threat.

Getting ready for my heat it crossed my mind for a moment to try this unorthodox technique, but pride intercepted the idea. If I couldn't make it by surfing properly, then I wouldn't make it at all.

As the field of almost a hundred began to whittle down, the usual mutinous atmosphere began to ferment. By half-eleven several surfers had uttered one of the essential lines, without which a British surf contest is not officially underway:

'Beginning to wonder why I fuckin' bothered with this crap…'

This was followed, of course, by a chorus of approval:

'Nah, me neither. Too cold. Shite waves. Every other weekend sportsman in the country's feeling more comfortable than us right now, I bet you.'

'Got that right, like.'

As always a round of silence followed it, before, 'When's your next heat then?'

'Dunno. You?'

Shrug of shoulders. 'Might go look in a minute.'

We all knew when our next heats were, but this is part of the bullshit banter that everyone loves to fall comfortably into.

Round two was more of the same, with each of us visitors sneaking through before Terry announced that the field had been sufficiently whittled down to finish the event that day (without needing the Sunday), as long as things kept going this smoothly. It would of course mean using every second of daylight, as well as pushing the presentation well into the evening. All convinced of our chances, this sounded like a plan, and as two more rounds passed by without hiccup all three of us began to develop the tunnel vision of surfers who are getting into a proper contest rhythm. (While Andrew and Al had also begun thinking about their chances of scooping a team prize.)

That's a common experience for many competitive surfers – that rhythm as the heats get closer and more serious in nature – but not for me. I'd been involved in the business end of a contest draw far too seldom for my liking and was really relishing a quarter-final heat in marginally improving conditions.

High tide had pulled a little more water over what precious little sandbanks existed here, meaning small gaps had started to show in the total close-outs of the early rounds. It was still verging on the unsurfable, but every now and then, if you positioned yourself intelligently, it was possible to sneak on to a little bit of running wave face and some were even affording the opportunity to do a couple of half-decent manoeuvres.

I squeezed, wincing with cold, into my soaking wetsuit for what would, either way, be the last time that day. If I got through this heat, the semi would follow so quickly it wasn't worth coming back up to the car to get changed.

During the afternoon, for some inexplicable reason, Terry had decided to move the contest area a hundred yards north along the beach. With every point along the sands producing identical waves, the only excuse I could see for this was that the rising tide had brought the surfers closer to the judges. Perhaps wanting to keep things difficult, he'd thought it fit to move us further away again.

Adding to the rather peculiar judging situation, it was also threatening to get dark at the earliest possible moment. The sun had barely come up at all that day anyway and therefore slipping from day back to night seemed something the sky was ready to do as and when it pleased – regardless of whether or not Terry had finished running the event.

As it happened, I soon realised that even the onset of night wouldn't dissuade him. Calling everything off prematurely for bad light was beginning to look like a real possibility as I walked past the misted-up windscreen of the van through which the judges intended to watch, and hopefully reward, my imminent demolition of the waves below. I paused to ask them for the heat times and wave-count limit, causing one of the judges to wind a side window down – about which he was less than pleased. A whiff of something funky caught my nostrils as smoke poured out of the cockpit, and I immediately realised why he resented the interruption.

'Er, sorry,' I said, before I posed my contest questions.

'Dunno,' was the reply.

'I see. And any idea what colour I am?' I asked – referring to the vests that competitors would wear over their wetsuits in a heat, in order to allow the judges to distinguish between them impartially.

'Nope. Ask Terry.'

'Where is he?'

'No idea.'

Someone had ridden a wave during this conversation without being scored – as a result of my enquiry – but it was Al so I didn't mind. We'd reached the stage at which he was now a rival, and would probably be just as happy himself to throw loyalty out the window.

Terry, as luck would have it, was at the water's edge. He seemed the most in control he'd been all day as he handed me a white vest (second only in visibility to the red one – so a good one to draw in this impending twilight) and warned me that my heat was starting in fifty seconds. This was nowhere near enough time to get back out, but it didn't matter as none of the other three guys in my heat had made it down yet either.

I magnanimously accepted the vest and started paddling out to surf against myself for a place in the semi-finals; a reasonably inviting prospect.

As dusk enveloped us all, I took off on my first wave and stuck in two turns as well as a few wiggles in the white water. Encouraged by a good start, I paddled back out and repeated the process a few more times – before two of my other competitors eventually began making their way out about halfway through the heat. Two other surfers, meanwhile, had drifted into the line-up, both on longboards, both barely able to paddle in a straight line let alone ride waves. Very inexperienced surfers are often the hardest to deal with when they get stuck in a drift and arrive in your heat so, not wanting any kind of run-in, I made my way a little further up the beach.

It was at about the halfway point in the heat that I saw a pair of headlights come on back at the car park. This, I would later learn, was the judges attempting to improve their ability to see the line-up. Even if it had worked though, I'm not sure if it would have done anything to the result – which with only a few minutes to go was obviously going to go in my favour. As heats went, I'd surfed a blinder, steadily building an account of solid waves. There was another guy in the heat from Plymouth Uni, who I was certain had also advanced, while the other two had picked up nothing after their late arrival. One of them was a local – one of the 'students' Terry had admitted into the event because they were probably studying an A level one night a week in a local college, but it didn't matter – both had been comprehensively beaten. Or so we thought.

Walking back up the beach to turn our vests in to Terry, the Plymouth surfer cemented my ideas.

'What d'you reckon then, mate? You and me through in that one, eh? Looks like those two didn't catch anything...'

'Yeah, seems that way,' I confirmed. 'We managed to stay clear of the free surfers too, eh?' I nodded dismissively towards the two beginners who'd floated through the line-up – one of whom was also making his way in to the beach with the two local competitors.

We stopped to talk for a minute, watching the waves we expected to be paddling back into shortly, generally feeling pretty happy with things. This allowed the other surfers to make their way past us, to be the first to hear from Terry the results that had apparently already been radioed down from the judges' van. When the beginner clenched his fist in glory and shook Terry's hand, we realised something a little untoward was going on.

'What's he on?' I laughed, as we neared the contest director, who was gesturing urgently for our vests. In the darkening evening, I spotted something awkward in his eyes.

'Got the result?'

'Yeah, er, hard lines, fellas,' he replied.

'Sorry – come again?' I said in disbelief.

'Great surfing, boys. I'm sorry, though. It's so competitive at this stage, eh? You must be really pleased anyway.'

'You what?'

'Great run you were on. It's those two over there who made it this time, though. Close heat.'

My jaw dropped with indignant horror. He was pointing at the longboarder that had drifted into the contest area and who'd made us laugh by that fist clench only a moment ago. I'd seen the guy paddle into a wave and stand up for about half a second before falling off the nose. Not only was he not even part of the event, but this guy could barely surf – and that's being kind.

'He wasn't in the heat,' I said.

'No, no, what we do, you see,' Terry smiled placidly, 'is we run a ranking system so he came in through another heat. We didn't have a spare vest to judge him in, so he was written down as black on the judges' sheets.' The colour system existed to foster anonymous judging, in theory. The 'surfer in black' was so named because he wasn't wearing any colour

– which as far as I was concerned meant he wasn't in the event.

I was ready to throw a tantrum. 'In *black*?'

'Aye, you know – like a fifth man.'

'But only four people had qualified for that heat? Who was he?'

'No. There were five out there. Hard lines, like I said. Normally we put three competitors through to the next round from a five-man heat, but coz we're short on time it's only gonna be two today. Sorry, boys. We'll have a fun night tonight, though. Beer's cheap again!'

I knew beyond a shadow of a doubt that this was a debacle.

'What are we gonna do?' I asked the Plymouth surfer. He just shrugged his shoulders and said he'd heard of this kind of thing happening here before.

'But we can't let them pull this shit,' I pleaded.

'What option have we got?'

'But it's a complete *fix*!' I yelled.

I wanted to smash something, to hit someone or to throw a tirade of abuse, but the fact that I was stuck on a beach I hardly knew robbed me of the confidence I needed. Instead I ran back to the car park, past the judges (who were now on the beers too), to find Al and Andrew – maybe if we all got together to file some kind of complaint...

They were both dressed again, with their surfing stuff packed away.

'What's going on? Aren't you still in?' I asked.

'Nope,' Andrew frowned. 'We're both very much *not* still in. Al just got skunked by the worst judging decision ever made, while I missed my heat because it came forward half an hour.'

By now I realised we'd been had.

'They're down to the semis now and it's locals only left in the event.' Andrew folded his arms, resigned to what had happened. 'We've been done over. It's our fault for coming here and taking it so seriously. Not only is the joke on us, but we're helping make it funnier too.'

He was right – there was nothing we could do. All options available to us would run to dead ends. Taking off home in a mood would make us look like spoilt prima donnas from the photo-slut, big-business surf towns, where everyone supposedly surfed for image and success came easily. Staying and playing along with it all would be humiliating, not to mention lining Terry's pockets further. Andrew suggested, half-seriously, that we stick around, get steaming drunk and pick a fight – but even that desperate measure would surely result in us simply getting a hiding. The facts were simple: we'd trekked into parts of Britain that didn't have a surfing establishment in an attempt to clean up at the prize-giving and were being sent home with our tails between our legs.

'Sod it,' I said, opening my boot and throwing my board over the passenger seat. 'I'm getting changed and gonna go watch the final. Then I'm driving home to laugh about it tomorrow morning in Rest Bay with my mates, while remembering what surfing's really about.'

'Easy now,' Al laughed. 'Dunno about the watching the final bit...'

'Why not?'

'Well, I mean, it's not exactly the ASP World Tour out there, is it? And you did say the guy who won it last year allegedly sealed it with some kind of odd falling-off thing that Terry didn't know how to describe. You know dodgy judging happens in places like this. And don't forget with the tide dropping out it's about a mile back to the water's edge, which is the only place you're gonna see anything from.' Al had a point.

'Fair enough. Maybe I'll just go now then.'

It was Andrew who came up with a fitting compromise though.

'Nah – let's just get the grandstand view from here,' he suggested, smirking. 'It's fuckin' freezing anyway, so let's just hang out in the cars with the heaters running and watch what we can. I mean, if it's good enough for the judges…' Turning his key, his old estate spluttered, struggling to come to life in the cold, before revving triumphantly. He lifted the front seats forward and invited me to jump in.

It was ridiculous but, as if the ceremony of it would somehow make a difference, we settled down to try and observe the remaining surfing. The dark was now so absorbing that headlights actually made it harder to see. We turned them off again and spent the last half hour of the day – which was supposed to have been our swan song together – peering farcically in the direction of the sea. Instead of revelling in the success we'd expected to be our entitlement, we shivered, listening to the drunken giggles of the judges as they apparently ignored any idea of there being a final in the water in front of them.

This was actually the perfect way to see out the last moments of the silliest surfing contest yet to be found in this country of bizarre events and wacky surf clubs. Participating in that final would have been nowhere near as much fun.

And anyway we wanted to stick around to root for the new event favourite; the mysterious longboarder who had dispatched me, the uber-competitive wannabe, so calmly in the quarters.

'I reckon he's got the win in the bag,' said Andrew, gesturing into the gloom through which even the shoreline was now barely discernable. 'There was something about him, man. You could see that he was a winner from the off. He's given you your medicine and now he's gonna nail the rest of the field as well.'

Naturally, he did nothing much. We were backing the wrong silhouette – as we had been all weekend, for that matter.

Who the eventual winner was, we did not stick around to witness; a long, dark drive back through the winter night beckoning instead. The roads wound slowly away from Newgale's beaches and their bubble. Time seemed to slow, before empty dual carriageways flanked by farmland began to be punctuated by roundabouts and retail outlets. Everything about those reaches of West Wales felt designed to make the place appear isolated and remote, especially as winter set in. The car heaters offered consolation, as the lights of Carmarthen passed by to my left and then Cross Hands with its infamous McDonald's – whose curved tables and taunting comfort food had provided the setting for so many melancholy post-Nationals debriefs. This time I didn't even stop.

Andrew and Al whizzed past me as the M4 finally started – they had hours further to drive than me. From here the riveted, flaming illuminations of Port Talbot's vast steelworks and coke furnaces began the alluring countdown to home

– placing a time limit on what had been a reflective drive through the encroaching cold.

If anything, I thought, as these sights I knew by heart drew me towards the exit for Porthcawl and home, this could be yet another trip to add to the list of those that served to remind me how removed from the day-to-day routine I could still get, even in my own country, and of the insignificance of my surfing community once you were only a few miles away from it. It also made me wonder, as so often before, about the apparent futility of trying to compete sometimes – until I started chuckling aloud to myself about the comical improbability of where I'd just been and what had happened there.

Since then I had of course repeated yet more similar drives back from West Wales with the whole range of post-competition emotions (minus the ecstasy of victory, of course). But that trip to Nolton Haven and Newgale remained in my memory as a classic case of that quandary I'd lived with for so long in my life as a British surfer. That struggle for meaning; which, in the next few months of my life, I was hoping would finally start to get me somewhere.

As memory allowed my understanding of that trip to sharpen, I realised that, for all the humour and folly of that naïve jaunt taken in search of what at best would have merely been an unfulfilling ego-boost, there was one thing I'd completely forgotten to do and that was appreciate the adventure, change of scenery and break from the norm that such a trip could offer. If the chance to go to an event like that ever arose again, I needed to make more of it.

Adventure, mishap and discovery were always closer and more readily available than first presumed. I just needed to remember that – and to be willing to look for it.

CHAPTER 5
CARDIFF'S SUBURBAN SECRET SPOT

Don't get too excited here – I can't tell you where this is on pain of death and several other fates that are probably even worse. It's the rules when you talk about secret spots, and no matter what is dangled in front of me there are certain surf spots in the UK that it would be virtually criminal to give away the vitals for. What I *can* tell you about, though, are the waves that I surfed one late winter's day in the city of Cardiff. You may blurt out at this point that there are no surf spots in Cardiff – and you'd be right. Almost.

A friend of mine claims to relish seeing the surprise on people's faces when he tells them Cardiff has a beach. But it does have one – albeit a sickly one filled with industrial pollution – and to throw you yet further off the scent, the surf spot I'm speaking of is nowhere near it. I'm talking about a second, even lesser-known one.

I've only surfed the wave, which I'll dub 'The House', once, but it remains one of the most memorable sessions I've ever had, due in most part to the circumstances in which the surfing took place.

It was when I was nineteen and I had just returned home from a long-haul trip somewhere tropical. A lot of my friends were in similar circumstances; spending their days either surfing or preparing for another trip by looking for work at a relaxed pace. For most of us it was about as good as we could imagine life to be, as long as there was the promise of another trip on the cards.

The day began as an exceptionally windy one. Despite the south-westerly gales, however, there wasn't quite enough swell to surf at some of Porthcawl's more sheltered spots. A wave that broke off the harbour wall, known as 'The Wedge' and effectively my home break as it was near to the street I grew up in, wasn't going to work – which meant that on this particular day the only real chance of surfing anything decent was to get out of town.

Another mate, who was saving to go away, had the afternoon off from his temporary job at the local day-care centre, and had turned up with a car and a full tank of petrol. The chap in question will go by the name of 'Marc' for the purpose of this story, as that was the name he later took when he became the central character in my book *Chasing Dean*, in which we followed hurricane surf across the US Eastern Seaboard.

That morning he had made a call to a mutual friend of ours, Rich Grove, who lived in Cardiff – which was about thirty miles up the coast in the wrong direction if you wanted to be a surfer. We'd got to know Rich as kids because he was always in the water in Porthcawl – so much so that he ended up being better than most of the locals our age. In the early days his mother, Val, used to come down and wait patiently for hours on end while he surfed – whatever the weather or time of day. After a little while Rich started staying at my house, and before long he was effectively an honorary Porthcawl boy. In return for their letting him stay at my house, Val would then save my parents the job of driving me to Cornish surf contests, before we all grew old enough to get around ourselves and started going slightly further afield together – Sri Lanka, California and Mexico for a start.

On this particular morning, however, Wales would have to do – and the wind swell that was on offer had us stumped for where to surf. Marc's first plan had been to try Llantwit Major, a short hop east, until he'd got a different idea from his phone call to Rich.

'Grovey reckons he knows a secret spot in Cardiff that's gonna break today,' Marc grinned as I opened the door to him. 'What d'you reckon? I dunno if I'm that keen to go on a wild goose chase. Llantwit could be all right in a bit. But he did seem pretty wound up about it.'

Looking back, I suppose it was a mark of our enthusiasm that we were so keen to try it out. To most Porthcawlies a day when there's nowhere to surf locally is taken as a day not to surf at all, especially when that day was perhaps the coldest in the January of what had already been a long, dark winter. Llantwit being 'all right' wasn't exactly the most tempting offer of surf ever laid down for someone, but that wasn't the way we did things then. Frozen wetsuits were folded into bin bags and stuffed in the back of Marc's mother's car, in preparation to go and find wherever along our coast would provide us with a rideable wave that day.

'I dunno though, man,' I said to him as we drove over the hill out of Porthcawl. 'I've been on a lot of surf trips with Richie Grove and I can't see any reason why he'd make something up.' Rich had mentioned this spot in Cardiff to me before a few times and I'd wanted to see it for myself. From the first occasion of my ever having stood up on a board, the idea of riding a wave some place new had always been one of the most exciting things I could think of.

'Oh well, let's go and take a look at Llan-*twat* and then decide,' Marc asserted. 'Grovey says he's gonna be in till twelve anyway, and kind of needs us for a lift to the beach. His folks are at work.' I love the selfishness of surfers – the thought of picking Rich up *before* checking Llantwit, so that he could join us if we decided to go in there instead, didn't occur to us for a second. He'd only come into the equation if it suited us. But that was always the deal when all any of us really cared about was our own wave-count.

Regardless, we ended up in his company not long later. After three-quarters of an hour's driving, only to spend ten minutes looking at a lacklustre and wind-ravaged point break, we decided to play this wild card. Llantwit's waves weren't any better than Porthcawl – and we had run out of options for sure.

Rich was delighted to see us: 'I could have told you drongos that Llantwit would be shit hours ago!' he grinned, opening his parents' front door to us and loading his stuff out of the porch and into the car. Only twenty-plus miles from home and this was now, for two of us, previously unsurfed territory.

'Right. Let's go, boys!' he cheered. 'This is gonna be sick; I can feel it. I'll show you the way.'

Here again I must be careful to omit the exact details regarding the whereabouts of where we headed next. Let's just say we left Rich's house on the outskirts of Cardiff, sneaking Marc's mother's car through a series of increasingly thinner lanes, until a couple of miles of farmland abruptly turned straight back into another of Cardiff's coastal suburbs.

Rich pointed out an unmarked lane again, which immediately plunged us into tunnels of trees, blocking the already weak winter light. Dead and rotten leaves lined the roadsides – nobody had swept them away since autumn – before a low railway bridge appeared like a gateway to another world. The forest around us thickened, turning the city centre, still only quarter of an hour behind, into a hazy memory.

A few big buildings appeared on our left, one with a 'Flat to Rent, Low Price' sign outside it, before a sharp drop-off indicated that there was ocean below. Marc parked the car onto a lip of turf and mud, and we waded through more dead leaves to peer through a layer of barren trees and an elevated view of rocky coastline. We tiptoed closer to the edge of a sharp drop until a reef set-up came into view, just as snowflakes began to fall. A near-vertical slope of forest lay between us and the water below, trees and foliage precariously clinging to land that looked as if it was ready to fall into the sea at any moment. To our left I could see from the movement of the sea surface that there was some kind of beach, hidden from view by more dense growth. There was no surf at all, but this seemed inconsequential to our guide in chief.

'Yep,' he confirmed, shaking with excitement. 'It's gonna be *on*.'

'You fuckin' what?' spat Marc.

'It's gonna pump boys. I'm so amped. Come on, let's suit up.'

'Hang on,' Marc interrupted, putting his hand on the boot firmly and dismissively just as Rich went to lift it and get his suit. 'There's no surf at all. Like *no surf* – not small, not even tiny. It's F-L-A-T, *flat*!'

'So?'

'He's right, Rich,' I added.

'It don't matter, boys,' came the reply. 'I promise you this spot is gonna fire any minute now.'

Despite our sceptical faces, Rich pressed on by explaining to us the unique nature of the spot we were dealing with. Apparently it pulled swell in through the Bristol Channel on a big tide, provided the wind was blowing behind it at exactly the right angle. It needed a big south-westerly, whereupon the swell size would hardly matter. The important factor was the wind fetch, and whether a sustained breeze could line itself up in precisely the same direction as the tide. According to Rich, the sea would soon surge around the little headland and in front of a rocky outcrop that had broken off to form a small island. When that happened it would be bringing with it an hour of stored wind swell, pouring over the soon-to-be-submerged reef. Today, apparently, had just that combination of conditions, and if we didn't get changed now the surf spot would certainly start breaking without us, from nothing. As if that wasn't hard enough to believe, Rich also reckoned it would return to being flat by high tide – meaning hardly anyone else who mattered had ever seen the place breaking.

Like I say, our big dilemma was whether to believe him. Surely this had to be a big wind-up designed to make us look like a pair of tools. Rich had been surfing Llantwit a bit more lately and a friendly yet significant turf war existed between there and Porthcawl, so to me it wasn't that far-fetched that he'd been cajoled into some kind of naughty prank. Maybe the Llantwit crew had told him to stitch us up in return for being welcomed in their line-ups. Perhaps 'Vaughanie', their self-proclaimed ringleader, was waiting below with a camera to snap pics of the Porthcawl boys in their winter wetsuits, waiting for swell on a flat beach in the middle of Cardiff.

I tried to dismiss such paranoid ideas. This was a good friend of mine, who I knew we could trust... or could we?

'I want to see you halfway into your suit before I start,' Marc demanded.

'Fine,' Rich grinned back. 'See me get shacked out of my fuckin' mind before you bell-ends are even in the water!' If this was a joke, he was doing a good job of concealing it.

Marc remained sceptical, but this was enough for me. I'd seen enough to know Rich meant business here, and it seemed a worthwhile risk.

Knowing what was in store, and having a dry, warm and accommodating wetsuit due to living away from the beach, Rich wasted no time at all in readying himself and starting to scale the narrow, mossy path down to the water's edge. A derelict-looking concrete gateway led on to a trail that Rich started to deftly negotiate, half sliding, half skipping through frozen mud, smooth, foot-worn stone and rotting trees. Once he got to the beach he started jogging on the spot and stretching, just waiting for what still looked like nothing.

Sleet was thickening to snow and starting to stick as I pulled my neoprene gloves and hat on, blowing thick steam in front of me with every breath. A frozen lump of wax jarred noisily with my board as I tried to rub a little extra traction on. Marc locked the car up and together we started to make our own way down to the cola-coloured Cardiff sea. Although in the lee of Wales's biggest city, the place felt completely deserted, except for a few caravans tucked into the hill, boarded up and hibernating.

At the bottom of the trail we stepped out onto a narrow, gravel bay. Invisible from the car was the final piece of backdrop from which we gave the spot its name: a grand, deserted and crumbling house slowly sinking back into the headland, behind which it had once found refuge from the angry winter seas. Noble and longstanding, the house peered over the patch of rock we were about to surf, its probable ghosts able to watch us from the windows.

'Maybe we have got an audience,' I noted to Marc, pointing up at the structure. 'Albeit a supernatural one.'

By the time we were at the shoreline the tide had made its leap over the reef, just as Rich had predicted, encouraging him to paddle out ahead of us. It still looked odd, watching him sitting in a dormant ocean. Even the spirits would struggle to make sense of this, although they'd probably seen him do it before, alone, many times.

He bobbed for a few minutes, a black dot of neoprene waiting, calm and serene. Then, as if a switch in the ocean had been flicked, a rapid rip appeared out of nowhere, visibly pushing water around the headland – and with it a row of waves was released from the turbulent ocean behind, making their way to the shore.

Adept and experienced in this rarest of surf spots, Rich knew exactly where to sit and was on the first wave, which began bowling around the reef as good as anywhere in Porthcawl, peeling to the right at perfect pace. With a snappy, quick-footed style, he made a lurching drop and drove a sharp downwards turn mid-face, narrowly missing a gurgling tube. He emerged back on the open wall and smacked in three explosive turns, before pulling off into the flats behind with a hoot and a thumbs-up in our direction. Out of nowhere, incredible surf had instantly materialised.

My and Marc's reluctance disappeared immediately; we couldn't paddle out quickly enough. In this little nook in the coastline, the wind was minimal, sheltered by a headland to our west, and the frigid brown water was making the hollow waves appear dark but cosy. We were still only halfway out when Rich stroked in to another one, this time getting the take-off just right and slipping into a tight tube, which he expertly threaded to escape yards in front of us. Using his momentum he floated, still standing, way out into the channel, through yet more thin snowflakes falling softly out of a watery grey sky. Despite the poor daylight, the silhouette of the house remained distinctly visible in the background.

'Now d'you believe me, boys?' he bellowed. 'NOW D'YOU BELIEVE ME?'

The swell on offer was uneven and inconsistent across the rest of the coast that day, but here the waves were stacking up enticingly with hardly any time to wait between sets – which was ideal as it made it easier to keep warm by staying busy. When I arrived in the line-up, although I had to wait for Rich to take his turn as thanks for bringing us here, it wasn't long before I was on one myself: a left-hander off an A-frame peak that had also offered Marc a right.

I'm hopeless at pulling in to the tube when grabbing rail (holding on to your outside edge while dropping your back knee onto the deck). Known as 'pig-dogging', this is what you usually need to do in order to have any chance of barrel riding with your back to the wave, as it enables you to fit the shape of a tube without being face-on. But, unless you know how to do it properly, pig-dogging severely limits your balance, which is why it's a lot harder than getting tubed on your 'front side'. As a result I barely have any memories at all of decent tubes when riding to my left, or 'back side'.

But this was one of them.

As I paddled for the wave it had looked innocuous, but once I went over the ledge the bottom dropped straight out. Without really knowing it, I promptly found myself slouching in a cavern of dense, freezing water. In fact, with hindsight I think it was actually due to reading the wave wrongly that I was able to get into this position. If I'd known how quickly this spot made the lip lurch forward at take-off, I'd probably have ridden it more cautiously, but being blissfully unaware of the danger had allowed me to misjudge my way into a brilliant bit of tube riding.

It felt great for that instant – until everything went alarmingly wrong. The wave took another turn, just as I was harbouring fantasies of actually making it out of the tube, and I was flicked forward into the lip, which promptly smashed me downwards for a face-first embrace with the reef.

Layers of winter wetsuit can pad you against this kind of thing though, and, as reefs come, this was a soft one – flat patches of slippery stone, with none of the sharp edges that lined the reef breaks at home. So it was with an invigorated soul that I resurfaced, yelling with delight at the view I'd just had, before powering my way back to the line-up, itching to catch another.

'See what I mean?' Rich was grinning. 'This is an awesome wave, boys, and no fucker knows about it. No one!' He was granted a short break between sets to repeat various combinations of this comment, before another wave bent its way in towards us and he pushed himself over the ledge and into another white-knuckle ride. Behind it, of course, were more identical, warping walls of water – too many waves for only three friends to share.

More snow began to fall as we continued swapping waves, each cheering or hooting the others when a good one came through. Tucked neatly in the lee of a headland, the wind was diverted away from us, adding to our little bubble of perfection. I looked around, at the house with its sheets of settling snow, to the trees above that were swaying in a breeze that everyone but us could feel. Only a few hundred yards from the shoreline, the real world continued to be bombarded by the gales blowing their way across South Wales, while we were surfing glassy A-frames.

The oddness of this rare surf was added to by the weather and timescale. It remains the only time I've ever seen it snow during such strong sea breezes, and all along we knew with every wave that, as Rich had promised, the spot could suddenly be about to stop, leaving this moment behind us for good. This awareness can sharpen the clarity of wave riding and its memories, and the sight of that lip pitching over me, obscuring the whitening headland and its lonely house from view, will remain seared in my mind.

It was a sight I would get a good chance to memorise during the hour or so that remained of our session, during which all three of us were completely absorbed by the process of poaching waves and trying to thread tube after tube of Cardiff sea water. And that was indeed what it felt like. Poaching. Taking something that wasn't supposed to be there for us. We needed to act fast, to fill our boots, until the opportunity vanished.

When it inevitably did just that, none of us complained. Impervious to the freezing, late afternoon, we giggled and yelled our way back to the car. It was utterly surreal for me to see a surf spot appear and disappear in the manner that 'The House' did that day, and in the end it served to remind me just how unfathomable the ocean was in its ways.

Driving back to the city, with the heaters of Marc's car turned to their highest setting, Rich summed it up. 'I love this place. That was my home break back there, boys. Hardly ever breaks. Keeps itself to itself; it's not flashy, like, doesn't try to advertise itself, but just waits for its moment and then blows you away.'

'Bit like you, Rich,' Marc pointed out.

'If you say so. It wasn't what I was getting at, like.'

I laughed. It was Rich's day, for sure. For once, after years of being a guest in our waters, he'd got to welcome us to his own local surf spot.

'I have to say though, boys... either of you tell anyone where that was,' he added, 'and I'll never speak to you again.'

'Can we say it's in Cardiff?' I asked, straining my voice to be heard over the heaters.

'Yeah, but that's it. Otherwise I'll have to start sharing my surfs here with people I don't know, and I'm not up for that one fuckin' bit. Tell the story, by all means. But keep this place a secret – at any cost.'

'OK. No worries.' We both offered our promises, although it wasn't as if anyone else was ever going to successfully work this place out without Rich's help, anyway.

'It has to be said, see,' he added. 'I've kept this place to myself for yonks, like. Now you boys have to do the same.'

'We will, man, for sure,' I repeated.

Years later, I'm going to have to apologise to you for what I'm leaving out of this story as a result.

But I don't break promises, see.

CHAPTER 6
CHASING BILL: CORNWALL (PART ONE)

Cornwall has always represented to me a gloomier side of UK surfing. If you grow up outside of the place, aspiring to surf as well as people from there, then a thinly veiled resentment of the Cornish surf scene is in your nature. It's partly down to straightforward wave envy, of course, but some of the more bitter feelings have their roots in a sense of injustice, too.

Despite having the most consistent waves in the southern half of Britain and lovely blue water most of the year – as opposed to the greys, greens and browns of the rest of the coasts – Newquay will forever be known as the town that really brought the rat race to surfing. It's the hub of the industry and the point at which the polluted river of money pours into the pure ocean of surf stoke. The surf mags are there, the photographers, the contests, the companies, the supermarket-sized clothing emporiums and the groupies. As a result, to a lot of Welsh surfers it often feels like a place that played the bullshit part of the surf game really well. The rumour always went that an upcoming Newquay surfer could get just as much coverage and success as he or she would by winning a contest, by simply having a good 'corporate appearance' (such a thing does exist in surfing) and a mobile full of photographers' numbers.

And yet, throughout my journeys as a surfer, good friends have always enjoyed going there; one of whom was Rich Grove.

Some ten years after he took me to his secret backyard reef break, Rich wound up living in Cornwall, just outside Newquay. In the time that had passed he'd spent a couple of years in Australia renting an apartment by Queensland's world famous 'Superbank', had tried Raglan in New Zealand and indeed the snowy hills of Colorado – as well as sojourning in Indonesia at length several times. So why settle in Cornwall? It didn't make sense to me.

While it wasn't my job to question his decision, it was well within my remit to take advantage of it. So when he returned to Wales for a few months while waiting for a carpentry job to begin back in Falmouth, I suggested we road-trip around Cornwall. He could be my guide and help me understand the face of 'Kernow' that I'd missed by always going straight to Newquay on the busiest weekends of the year in order to get knocked out of contests early.

'Sweet idea,' he drawled down the phone to me. 'Just what the doctor ordered. There's a sick swell running this weekend as well.'

He was right. I'd seen it too. We had both been monitoring the same online surf reports – Magic Seaweed, Scripps Institute and the FNMOC models used by the Navy – along with pretty much every other surfer in Britain. In fact, the swell expected over the coming weekend was not just a regular early autumn storm. It was one of the few Atlantic hurricanes to send waves to Britain in years. Hurricane Bill was in the vicinity.

Rich immediately dubbed the mission 'Chasing Bill'; our own version of the trip I'd taken with Marc along the US East Coast, which was traditionally the hurricane surfing Mecca of the world.

Bill looked like he had the potential to spin his own way into surfing folklore, too.

'Cornwall will turn on as good as anywhere when a deep one swings by,' Rich urged. 'Whatever it does, there's gonna be surf somewhere. We'll just crash in the car, or if we need to call on some of my mates then we can do that too. I'm amping just thinking about it.' His enthusiasm and stoke were catching on with me too.

The next morning I grabbed him from his parents' house in Cardiff and we made for the M5 to the south-west, in my case feeling more expectant than ever before about driving in search of surf in Britain.

It helped that, after a wet summer, we were facing a day of blistering sunshine, which filled the fields and meadows of Somerset and Devon with colour – the product of what had been an August of rains and warm nights. The first frosts of the year were still weeks away and by mid-morning the windows were down as we cruised the three-lane motorway under blue skies. The lively sea temperatures of North Cornwall would feel welcoming after donning dry wetsuits in a sunny car park. It was now a matter of working out where to stop for surf number one of what we were hoping would be a feeding frenzy of waves.

The only thing going against us was the wind. Although it was moving softly over the shores, there was a more local storm near to the coasts that was threatening to dilute the power of Bill's more long-range swell.

'We need to surf somewhere that the swell has to bend into,' Rich explained. 'That'll clean it up. Somewhere like Great Western, but *not* Great Western.' Most surfers loved to hate this beach, one of Newquay's north-facing beaches, for being perhaps too obvious an option in a westerly wind.

'Yeah, you got that right,' I confirmed. One thing I'd garnered some expertise in (during the research for *Chasing Dean*) was the acquisition of hurricane surf. If a counter- or cross-swell came in, you needed to find somewhere that the bigger hurricane waves could wrap into, leaving the other stuff behind – otherwise the surf would get messy and you'd end up chasing your tail trying to pick up unpredictable set-waves in odd conditions.

It was essentially a filter effect. Hitting a headland and turning around a corner in a coastline was something only the most powerful waves would survive. An obstacle like that would intercept most mediocre waves, but a hurricane swell would still make the refraction with its juice intact. With the background slosh from the local swell getting held back, a 'wraparound' spot – if we could find one – would benefit from this natural sieving away of the unrefined surf.

We settled on Harlyn Bay, which was usually a sheltered beach break on the reverse side of the peninsular of land that was home to the better-known Constantine Bay.

'Head to Padstow,' he instructed me, our destination being only a few miles from there.

Normally, Harlyn was not a beach you'd naturally head to for surf – but this was not a normal swell and Rich reckoned we didn't need to see it to know Constantine and anywhere else west-facing would be a mess.

As I guided my Citroën C3 (a clear sign of age, it was the first car I'd ever owned that was less than ten years old) through the final lanes approaching the shoreline, I realised how few of my numerous Cornish memories actually involved good surf. Most of my experiences of Britain's most wave-rich county were based around gloomy contests under grey skies, where I was doomed to lose and then get stuck in town while waiting for whoever I'd travelled down with to be ready to leave. And of the memories that didn't revolve around competing, most were of pointless visits to try and schmooze within the surf industry: sponsor runs, errands for friends who had scored jobs as sales reps or 'working lunches' with media brokers.

Of course, some of my previous Cornwall trips had been fun: the *real* UK Student Championships for one. Then there had been the first time I'd ever seen the ASP World Tour on British shores while on a camping trip with Rich's family. But, in well over a decade of coming to Cornwall, I was struggling to think of the times I'd been greeted with surf of real quality.

That wasn't going to be the case any more.

Harlyn Bay was firing. Turquoise, A-frame peaks, groomed by a steady and sweetly accurate offshore wind, were folding the length of the beach – peeling off methodically, mechanically and at a dream pace for speedy, playful surfing. Finally I was going to experience the other face of Cornwall, and it felt deserved.

Here – a rarity to be savoured – was pumping British surf in gorgeous glassy conditions. Who needed Australia, California, France? Today this was as good a place as any to be a surfer.

After a quick glimpse of the perfection on offer, a row of trees obscured the view, which allowed me to concentrate on parking behind the Harlyn Inn pub.

'Beers in there later, butt,' Rich grinned, 'to help us nod off in the car ready for a dawnie tomorrow.'

'Do we have to buy a ticket to park here while we surf?'

'Dunno. Your problem, that one. I'm in there.'

Rich grabbed his inside-out wetsuit and began beating out the sand from his last session, before turning it through and reaching for his towel. Another surfer was changing in the car next to me. He leaned over to answer my question:

'Nah, man. Free parking. You just need to buy a pint later. They're cool about sleeping in cars, too.'

Not wanting to lag behind my friend, who at times could well be the keenest surfer on earth, I took this to be assurance enough and rummaged for my own suit.

Getting changed in sunshine, waxing up slowly and then being able to leisurely walk with your wetsuit undone around your waist to a line-up of perfect peaks is a treat anywhere. It gives you time to contemplate the bliss of what's on offer. As we neared the edge of the water, I watched wave after wave crackle along. There seemed hardly any crowd for what were already some of the best surfing conditions I'd seen in this part of the world.

'Where are they all?' I asked Rich.

'Getting frustrated trying to surf somewhere else that's picking up the wind swell,' he gloated. 'I didn't have a clue it would be like this here. Just thought it was worth a look. Got to 'fess up now, man. This was just a lucky guess.'

He winked.

'Whatever,' I replied. 'Good call, anyway.'

At the eastern end of the beach, where we began wading in, a half-submerged rock was holding up a consistent series of fast right-handers, with almost no paddle-out needed. The two other surfers seemed mellow enough, considering our arrival in the line-up had effectively doubled the crowd – and I promptly saw why. The surf was far too good to worry about such things.

The elder of the pair paddled for a shoulder-high wedge just as I arrived out back – a wave so obviously hollow that his moderate surfing ability was ample to get himself slotted into a dry tube. As he passed me with a look of trepidation, the cool lip slapped his sunburnt forehead, throwing him off as the rest of the wave shut down teasingly.

I waited for him to re-emerge. The delight in his face was immediately apparent, and I hooted over to him. If they kept on getting rides like that all day the locals were likely to be placated and in a good, sharing kind of mood – which would only help our own chances of getting a few.

Tauntingly, the ocean went into a lull in sets as soon as we arrived in the line-up, so I sat up on my board, feeling the sun, looking down at my feet clearly visible through the crystal water, and waited contentedly for the wave machine to turn back on.

Soon enough another pulse appeared on the horizon and a head-high peak made straight for me. After a long drive down and feeling a bit agitated by the sight of new shores and an alien beach, I had to really concentrate on holding back my excitement. Calm as I could, I paddled into it, popped up and tried to race high across the face, which was walling surprisingly quickly for a random beach break I'd never heard of. Dropping back down the wave, I aimed for the close-out section and tried to glide over it, part-freefalling into the flats in front. The wave bounced behind me as I landed with speed and turned to punch my way under the white water, popping up in the shallows with churned sand bubbling all around me. The momentum of wave riding was coursing through my veins.

Immediately behind me I saw Rich slide into one, trying for a quick tube before going into a series of playful turns with that familiar, zippy style of his, which I'd seen so many times in my life – but not enough in recent years.

'It's on!' he grinned, kicking out and wading towards me.

The scene was already set for a surf session that would etch itself into my memory. That balance of cool water and warm air, the magnetic pull of waves pitching over the abrupt sandbars and subsequent torrent of spray from offshore winds. Everything felt great – my board, my surfing and our prospects for a few days of back-to-basics road-tripping.

A few rides later, I realised that the waves also had enough open face on them to really enjoy trying to surf on rail as well; carving and cruising across open expanses of powerful moving water. Usually a fast-breaking beach break would require a lot of reflex surfing, as you tried to reach the next section before it closed out, but here the peaks were solid, sure of themselves and ideal for really ripping.

For Rich, it was also a chance to show me just how bloody good at surfing he'd become in the last few years. After holding back on his first few to limber up and get a feel for it all, he suddenly caught a smaller inside wave, with a gem of a section on it, and busted loose. I could see his eyes tracking the lip line, taking aim and then, as the wind lifted yet more spray off the breaking wave, he launched cleanly out of the water. His timing was perfect, and he soared through the air, turning gradually to land into a sideways slide across the white water. I was close enough to hear his feet squeaking against the rubber tail pad as he held the board neatly under his feet, using the wind for help.

I yelled my approval and spun around to catch another one myself. I finished up right next to him and, as we paddled out side by side, he gave me his verdict.

'This is it, man. Surf's pumpin', sun's out. These waves are good for trying anything.'

'For you maybe,' I pointed out. 'Since when d'you learn to do two-foot punts?'

'Dunno. Just tried one day and it worked. You should have a go.'

If only it were that easy.

One of the toughest – although highly enviable – decisions to have to make in surfing is the two-stop-one-stop option. When faced with epic waves you have to decide whether to surf once until you drop dead with hunger and fatigue, or to cut the first session off a little earlier, re-fuel, rest and then return for a second go.

In the rarest of good surfs, you can sometimes try to get away with both – to have your cake and eat it, as it were. And that is what Rich and I attempted to do that day in Harlyn.

We saw the first session through to the point where we could physically catch no more waves – during which Rich took the opportunity to put on a masterclass in aerial and fins-free surfing. I, meanwhile, stuck below the lip like a mere mortal, made do with enjoying the on-tap speed and flow offered by wave after wave of hurricane energy. With each turn I could feel myself sharpening, absorbing the power and rhythm of the swell into my soul.

Eventually the real world caught up, leaving me so hungry I could have considered eating Rich, or any other of the few locals in the water with us for that matter, not to mention being sunburnt and feeling devoid of shoulder muscles.

'Shall we head in?' I suggested.

'Yeah, man. I'm knackered now,' Rich agreed.

Taking one last wave in each, we ran aground and virtually crawled our way up the sand to dry off and recover from a marathon session. For a moment, I couldn't have cared if someone had said I'd never surf again. For a moment.

This was a swell that demanded our utmost commitment.

Within twenty minutes of drying off in the still sun-baked car park, we were already entertaining the idea of heading back out.

'I reckon we drive back to Padstow again,' Rich suggested. 'It'll be like five minutes. Get some nosh from Tesco – as well as some wine for me coz I need it to be able to sleep in a car – and then come back for an evening sesh, crash here, and be on it for the dawnie too.'

It sounded like a plan to me.

And so, after already exhausting the one-stop strategy, we set about trying to get another surf before the sun dropped on this first day of Hurricane Bill's payload.

For me, this first half day of an indefinite stay in 'Kernow' had already blown away my presumptions with its clear water, blue skies, sunshine, light winds, steaming surf, friendly faces and the thrill of a hurricane-chasing road trip. All of these were things I had convinced myself didn't exist without getting on a plane – and yet here they were. I'd even slept in my own bed that very same morning.

By coming here on a swell, with no contest in mind, no need to go anywhere near the town that need no longer be named, I had finally found a Cornwall that I could fall in love with.

Rich was delighted. 'Life's sweet down here eh, son? An' this is only the beginning, man. There's days of this swell left. Tons of *sick* surfing ahead. You won't wanna go home by the time we're done!'

Here's hoping, I thought.

CHAPTER 7
SURF CITY UK: STREAKERS, DRINKING INJURIES AND INFLATABLE CROCS

'The town that need no longer be named.'

No surfer serious about getting to know the British scene can really avoid going to Newquay at some point in their life. A bonanza of Cornish waves had perhaps helped me, for the moment, to start building warmer memories of the place.

And of all of these, my visits to the UK Student Championships stood head and shoulders above the rest. I've told you about the weak attempt to mimic this contest up in mid-Wales – but when it comes to the real thing, it is beyond doubt that the 'Student Nationals' is Britain's quirkiest surf contest. If there is ever a good time to go to Newquay, then this is surely it.

After a few years of hobbling and surf-tripping, and upon finally starting a university course, this contest had been one of the things I'd most looked forward to when deciding to become a student (along with being able to use the Student Loans Company to fund a few more years of hobbling and surf-tripping). The thought of descending on Britain's surf capital for a contest full of beginners and piss-heads appealed to my ego. It would be a chance to be a big fish in a small pond for once.

That said, 'small pond' is probably not the phrase. The Students does in fact boast the largest entry field of any surf contest in the world. The first year I did it the numbers were in excess of 400. That's a hell of a roster of fellow competitors to whittle your way through.

However, the portion of this 400 that would be able to surf to a competitive standard was minimal. Round one is famous for the legendary 'inflatable crocodile' – a tradition that someone invariably keeps alive each year by actually attempting to surf their heat on one. I'd heard rumours of people swigging Strongbow in the line-up, longboarding in fancy dress, surfing naked in February... the list goes on.

But as well as this, there was also the opportunity to be the talk of the town for a weekend if you could surf. A mate of mine studying at Bristol University had enjoyed rock-star treatment by making the final one year. However hard I tried to deny it, the Students event appealed to me as the chance to get on a roll in a big event without having to come up against any of the country's toughest athletes, who were all far too committed to their surfing to waste time doing degrees and the like. It's sad, I know, but when you put effort into competing and yet constantly lose, this attitude can be permitted from time to time.

Nevertheless, the first time I entered – in 2002 – I lost in the quarter-finals, on day two of three (and in the pouring rain of course), to someone who never did contests. While my memories of those events still lead to a chuckle, it remains without a doubt the most painful defeat of my life. Someone who didn't care had beaten me in the event I'd dreamed of doing well in.

Looking back, I think I deserved it though. Taking the Student Nationals seriously is against the rules. It's quite simply not in the spirit of the game.

I returned the following year, honouring the rules by being both more *and* less determined to get a result.

That second year became my favourite trip to date to the place that can't be named. It had been cold enough to keep the hordes away and yet the February sun had still decided to shine, bringing with it the antics for which the event was famous.

A solid swell had caused proceedings to get moved around the corner, from Fistral Beach to the more urban setting of Towan Beach. An ideal venue for this kind of contest. With Newquay's harbour sheltering its west, Towan was producing tame lines in the knee- to waist-height range, while the Walkabout pub (and later nightclub) allowed competitors a panoramic view of the east side of the town as it proudly overlooked the crescent-shaped bays of Tolcarne and Great Western. Participants could warm up between heats while gazing through the glass façade at either the beach below or the rows of older Cornish seaside homes to the left. There was also the day's Premiership football on screens all around and a beer promotion that allowed for plenty of boozing prior to surfing – another common habit at the Student Nationals. The less water-savvy the surfer, the more likely they were to get tanked up before paddling out.

It was no wonder, therefore, that the inflatable croc had emerged by midday. A soon-to-be-beatified novice from Durham Uni's C team had, in fact, decided to kill two birds with one stone. Not only had he turned out to his heat with a legendary croc for a surfboard; he'd kitted himself out in a Batman costume as well. The inflatable piece of puke-green watercraft was a beauty: about four feet long and it soon drew a crowd.

Usually at a surf contest it takes either a stacked final or the appearance of a famous pro to attract a crowd to the water's edge. But not at the Students. Reigning champ Al Mennie (the same Irish Al that I'd met at Nolton Haven) had managed to attend his heat with little more fanfare than a subtle mention from the announcer. But a quick headcount revealed that the kook on the croc had over eighty fans, cheering his every move from the sand.

Cheering his every move was a tough thing to do – because he didn't actually manage to get to his feet in fifteen minutes of trying. This was partly due to his cape almost drowning him – but largely down to the fact this was only his fourth ever attempt at surfing.

'Got to hand it to him though, eh mate?' one of his team-mates explained to me as I walked to the edge of the crowd.

'That's how you get noticed when you can't do air three-sixties.'

He'd certainly taught us more experienced competitors a lesson.

'I ought to try that,' Al joked. 'Except I'd look like an idiot. I think you need to be from Durham to pull that stuff off.'

'Never mind,' I reassured him. 'You'll just have to try an air three-sixty.'

The cape and croc wasn't the best of the antics I witnessed that weekend, however. Although highly entertaining, it was too obvious, too done before. Fool of the weekend had to go to either my friend Math or the person who gate-crashed the final.

Firstly, Math's moment of madness wasn't in the water – but it did end up being surfing related as it cost him his place in the semis.

Wanting to learn from last year's mistakes (namely taking things too seriously), I set off for Newquay's town centre and its bars and clubs that evening. The plan was to get everyone else who was still in the contest off their guard by being seen out and about, but then to slip away before Britain's most notorious night out could work its evil on my ability to surf the next day.

Despite their furiously denying it, this is usually the plan of everybody else that's in my situation – including Math. But he didn't need to go as far as the main strip before Newquay could work its evil on him. Not needing the persuasion of hundreds of drunk fellow students to derail his campaign, he was perfectly able to see to that himself.

'Did you know those white bollards are rugby-tackleable,' he explained to Dan, another one of Plymouth's hopefuls. 'In Wales they're all creased round the bottoms from when people try it. Watch…'

With that, he promptly threw himself horizontally at an illuminated rectangular white object on a nearby traffic island. True to his promise, it did indeed crumple, as if inflatable, allowing Math to roll over it and stand up triumphantly, as if he'd just dropped Jonny Wilkinson in front of a capacity-filled Millennium Stadium.

I spotted a glint in Dan's eye. 'Fantastic,' he said. 'Go on – do it again.'

It worked. Completely forgetting Dan was his opponent in tomorrow's first quarter-final, Math again lunged for the helpless device of traffic control. However this time I heard a slight crackling sound, mixed with a stomach-churning squelch.

There was a moment's silence before Math's agonised scream indeed confirmed that the noises had come from his shoulder.

With one of his toughest opponents now on the treatment table, it would be a slightly earlier passage to the semis for Dan. Bloody Plymouth Uni surfers; should never be trusted. They're like the Man United of the Student Championships – always over-confident and infinitely willing to indulge in the dark arts of psyching people out or persuading them to hurt themselves on the eve of a big heat. And whenever they need it, luck seems to be on their side too.

But Math should have known better. He had, only a few months before, been the proud recipient of a warning letter under the ASBO Act, when an off-duty policeman had happened upon him 'in an alcohol-enhanced state attacking roadside furniture'. What can you say?

Being the coward I am, I decided on this occasion to refrain from placing myself in harm's way, and after a few bottles of the lightest beer I could find, it was time to slip away. As I passed Burger King, with its bouncers standing in the night breeze trying to hide the fact they were nearly dying of cold, I began feeling smug, ready for a good night's sleep and a carb-heavy breakfast.

Half a day later I was reaping the rewards – walking down the steep hill and across Towan's paved beachfront promenade to collect a finalist's vest, passing the forlorn Math in his sling along the way.

It was at this point that I started to think seriously about things, with a satisfying feeling descending over me that the job had been done. I'd scraped through the rounds in which you weren't allowed too keen an attitude, to the final, along with the only three other surfers who'd maintained any state of sobriety last night. One of them was Al.

'Good to see you made it,' he said to me, as we arrived in the line-up and waited for the horn to signal the start.

'Yeah. Good luck, mate,' I offered as a response, as we both began frowning, ready to hassle each other to the death.

It was then that our thunder was yet again stolen by a member of the Durham crew.

A cheer arose from the beach, which even I wasn't vain enough to think for a moment could be for any of us, before I saw the spectators part to allow a naked man to run for the water's edge – carrying a surfboard under his arm.

Now, you may or may not have experienced the British seas in February – but in any case let me assure you that immersing yourself in them is something that, without a wetsuit, is indeed life-threatening. The cold is so intense it will cause muscles and vital organs to shut down – often very quickly. And if you are going to do it, it's worth bearing in mind that some very important body parts will shrink when coming into contact with the cold. This obviously hadn't bothered Durham Boy, who was displaying himself proudly to a crowd of students, at least half of which were female.

He had a mission, as could be seen from the furnace-like eyes with which he paddled towards us from the shoreline. For a moment it even occurred to me that he was going to hit one of us – but I then realised it was the look of a man who is in great agony, and who is applying every drop of energy to warding off hypothermia.

And, although it wasn't his main purpose, he had also succeeded in puncturing the tension we'd worked so hard to build up for the final. Al took some persuading at first.

'What are you doing?' he barked.

'What does it look like, mate?' came the reply – a voice trembling with the effects of too much cold.

'You're in real danger mate,' Al pointed out. 'You could drown.'

The reply was gold:

'I don't care, man! I just wanna get in the mags!'

At that point both Al and I cracked. Laughter took over and we realised we were in for a tough time regaining the competitive fire.

The moral victory went to the streaker. However, for the second time this weekend, a bout of Durham-born attention seeking was hindered by surfing ability. The naked hero had chosen to borrow a board from someone else that was too short for him (perhaps because he'd thought it would be more photogenic) and failed to get to his feet once he'd managed to stroke in to a wave. It was a shame, because he probably would have got a shot in a surf mag if it hadn't been for that.

So I may have done better this time around, but the competition element of the Student Nationals remains to this day almost surplus to the spirit of the weekend.

Since good waves are rare at such events, it's virtually obligatory for regulars at surf contests to be able to make their own entertainment, which has lead to a real tradition of great raconteurs. Someone always seems to take on the role of storyteller, or jester, beguiling the rest of the shivering, grumbling participants. It helps if the designated person has been eliminated, for some reason – maybe the need to get over defeat leads people to put on a light-hearted front.

Although I had a few tales myself stored up for such occasions, my rare run to the final had meant someone else needed to step up to the plate. Temporarily robbed of his surfing abilities, Math had spent the afternoon in the car park waiting for a lift home – and slowly sipping a few hair-of-the-dog cans of Stella Artois to numb the pain in his shoulder. On the sea wall at Towan, waiting for the results to come in and trying to warm up, Math entertained us with the story of how he gave one unknown Frenchman the worst day of his life by accident:

'We were in La Piste car park, you know, in Capbreton, the beach with all the German bunkers on it. D'you remember when they introduced those new toilets – the ones you had to pay twenty cents to use?'

His audience were nodding, so he continued. 'And they automatically self-wash too when you're done. Stink of disinfectant, like. That's coz they're designed for people to go in and out barefoot see, so the floors get cleaned. Well, me and Davo were staying there one night and we'd been sleeping in the car, like. The gendarmes had moved us in to the forest, but we'd come to check the surf first thing in the morning and I suddenly got the need to take a cack – like one of those really ferocious cacks that you only get from too much baguette and black coffee.'

I stopped loading my car, which was parked a few yards away, and stretched my hearing to take in what came next. Even though I'd heard the story a million times, I started grinning at what I knew was about to follow...

'I reckon I had about five minutes to play with before I had to go literally anywhere – the dunes or whatever. So anyway, I reached the bog and it's out of order. I was gutted.'

Math quelled a round of chuckling to keep going: 'It had some French message on it about the lights being broke and the door not shutting properly, I think. But it looked locked – there was a red light on anyway. So I thought maybe the sign was old, and it was working after all. I thought there was probably someone in there and I'd be able to go in a minute, like.

'So I wait there for a while – and I mean a while. Ages. Like nearly quarter of an hour, and all this time there's just volcanic movement going on in my guts – so much that I've got no chance of managing to walk anywhere else if I can't use this one.'

The laughter was building again. Toilet humour and surf contests are a perfect match. And this tale was as good as toilet humour got.

'Anyway, after ages I decide there's not anyone in there, so I opted to open it and see if it was possible to go in... I reached for the door, opened it like halfway, then by instinct I was like "Shit, sorry" and slammed it shut.

'There was this guy in there, see, on the fold-down seat. He was mid-log, man! I can only imagine it must have been a case of super-constipation. I mean, they do happen in France. He'd been in there twenty minutes, though, easy.

'Anyway, the look on his face, man. As soon as he realised the door was going to close he shot me this look, like "why have you done this to me?"

'It was only the lock that was broken, see. The second the door clipped closed there was this ticking sound, then a growl – you know, a deep, machine-like one.' Math paused to mimic the violent shaking he was describing. 'The ground literally rumbled as the self-cleaning system kicked in. And he was locked inside the whole time, man!

'Must be hell on earth. You've been sitting there for ages trying to force one out, like, and then all of a sudden the seat folds away behind you, you get locked in and the entire room starts spewing purple disinfectant everywhere.' He shook his head mournfully. 'Around there almost everyone is roughing it, so he probably had no spare clothes, nowhere to go and freshen up – apart from the sea, like.

'Somehow all of that made me able to move again. I ran all the way to the car and was like 'Davo, Davo man – we've got to get out of here NOW!'

He waited for the laughter to subside then signed off with, 'Worst thing I've ever done to anyone, man,' before he slid off the wall, winced with yet more shoulder pain, and started to walk towards contest control.

Retelling number one million and one had amused me just as much as the first. It got my mind off the imminent announcement of the final results – so much so that I was still grinning to myself as I stepped up to accept my bronze medal ten minutes later.

CHAPTER 8
CHASING BILL:
CORNWALL (PART TWO)

I suppose it was a measure of the different experiences available in Cornwall that these memories were returning to me as I sat on one of Padstow's sea walls. So what if most of my best experiences of this place involved fooling around on land? And anyway, I'd finally scored a good dose of great surf to add to the rest of it.

Seagulls gathered around me, swarming in off the low-tide sands to slurp up the remains of fish and chips cast aside by day trippers with dreams of Rick Stein seafood. Rich, obviously maturing in outlook a little himself, had shunned Tesco and McDonald's for the option of an authentic Cornish pasty – warmed and filled with ketchup. Weighing me down, its soporific effects were pushing surfing again to the back of my mind for the moment.

I looked at the row of shops and hotels, and the start of the winding streets behind them, across to the wide inlet of water bustling with boats cruising across the calm water. Here we were in the lee of the wind, and the view was one of total serenity. Here was the picture-perfect image of a quaint southern English coastal town. It did exist after all, if only for brief moments here and there.

'Good place to chill this, innit?' said Rich.

'Yeah. It's kind of… removed from surfing and the beach, isn't it?'

'Exactly. That's what I like about it. If we were eating and looking out to sea at Harlyn now, we'd be getting jumpy about going back in. This way we can properly chill and then go back in a bit feeling fresh to go and shred a few more.'

'In a bit though, eh?' I suggested.

'Oh, for sure. I'm just gonna lie here for a bit.'

He stepped off the wall to a bench that had now been left free as the town began to slow for the evening. The transition between the daytime and evening crowds had led to Padstow having a sleepy feel, while there was still enough warmth around to make you want to bask.

Rich stretched himself out, lying on his front, and pulled his hood over his head.

Turning to face back out over the Camel Estuary, I let my mind wander again.

For the next two days, this Cornish mini-trip continued to feel like a journey around my own past. Only this time it felt as if, by revisiting it all, I was able to see things from a point of view that had eluded me the first time.

This is the essence of travel. You have to be searching for something to get that sense of quest, and while we'd begun by simply looking for swell from Hurricane Bill and a chance to finally enjoy the simple act of surfing in Cornwall, I'd ended up finding something more.

Not only that, but I'd also, yet again, been reminded that this sense of self-discovery, that traveller's euphoria, existed as close to home as the other end of a car journey. You didn't need a cross-continental flight to somewhere that would put ink in your passport. The components were all here; old friends, a car, a swell – and a hurricane to chase.

'You wasted your time driving round Yankland, man!' Rich kept saying. 'Could have done it here, easy. I told you there's sick surf in Cornwall.'

It had taken barely twenty-four hours to get that idea over to me. A series of sessions in Harlyn Bay had already sated our appetites, despite the remnants of Bill blowing in and making almost every other inch of North Cornwall's waters resemble the swirling cauldrons of winter ferocity that normally render surfing impossible. Sheltered from the bigger gusts, and angled so as to receive the wind from an offshore direction, Harlyn continued to fire. Barrelling, A-frame waves the length of the beach had greeted us when we awoke in the Harlyn Inn car park on day three, nursing slight hangovers after an evening watching a ska band in the pub. A second night in the car had passed smoothly, so with sunburnt faces and aching shoulder blades from all the paddling, we logged one final session before two friends of Rich, 'Cheeks' and his girlfriend 'Coco', put us up on their floor in Truro.

As often happens when I crash on floors, I was up an hour earlier than everyone else, and took a walk through the town

– recognising little features and side streets here and there, but with no more recollection of when I'd previously been there.

Coco and Cheeks's place was in a neat little estate that was just beyond two objects that seemed to sum up this part of Cornwall. One was an ultra-modern skatepark, with various tailor-made rails and ramps being shredded to bits, even first thing in the morning, by a load of red-hot kids. And then there was the viaduct that loomed over both the estate and nearby park. Each of the stubbed streets showed evidence of surfer residents, with VW vans and ageing, stickered-up and salt-corroded cars – as well as the occasional board visible through a window or wetsuit draped over a washing line.

I walked up to the top of the hill, around a loop that passed the train station and dropped down towards a couple of curry houses and bars.

Everywhere I turned, something looked familiar.

It wasn't until we sat eating some Tesco-bought sushi for lunch, overlooking the riverbanks and marinas of one of Cornwall's only cosmopolitan areas, that Rich reminded me.

'We stayed with my mum's friends around here when we were like fourteen or something. After going to the Headworx Comp. Remember that?'

'Headworx? Oh yeah, *Headworx*! What happened to them?'

'Fuck knows. Good comp though, eh? You know, that was the first time we ever saw pros surf in Britain, wasn't it?'

Immediately I was there again, in the back seats of his mother's car, with us as teenagers winding his little sister up by continuously taking her Spice Girls tapes out of the communal Walkman and replacing them with NOFX, Good Riddance and Propagandhi.

The year he was referring to was 1997, we were seventeen, not fourteen as he remembered, and it was indeed the first time I ever saw professional surfers riding waves in the UK. Both of us had seen the pros in France before, but that wasn't nearly as impressive. We'd grown up with this belief that there was something exceptional about British surf – something exceptionally *bad*.

Watching the obligatory thousands of hours of Taylor Steele films (a groundbreaking San Diego-based surf-filmmaker) we'd seen some of the world's best surfers leap through the air, swoop through tubes and carve great scars in walls of powerful water. That was what happened everywhere else on earth, we thought. It was no surprise to us when on junior trips to continental Europe we got to see the same kind of surfing, and it would rub off a little too. But arriving home would always lead to a loss of momentum – your imagination would desert you, your turns would get slower, your timing slacker; you'd start to jerk horribly as you tried to milk non-existent speed out of impotent Bristol Channel wind swells. We didn't believe such surfing could be done in our waves – or at least that was our excuse.

Then came that three-hour drive in the back of Val's car to Newquay, whereupon, in knee-to-waist-high British summer surf, a large chunk of the world's best set about proving to us that an excuse was all it was.

At the Headworx Pro, in the hunt for vital World Qualifying Series points, we got to see, among others, Rob Machado, Cory Lopez and the two most formidable brother duos in modern surfing: CJ and Damien Hobgood and Bruce and Andy Irons.

A great thing about surfing, unlike almost any other sport, is that you can go and practise right alongside these demi-gods of professional sport. It's a free beach outside of the contest area and if they want to loosen up or test-ride a new board then it's in with the rest of the rabble.

As easily as I can still see Rich's little sister, Lizzie, fuming at the sound of surf punk usurping their mum's tape deck, I can still close my eyes and visualise a particular wave CJ Hobgood caught at low-tide Fistral. He got to his feet on an already broken wall of white water, which was backing off into deep water. On a wave I had always thought required the most earnest of frantic pumping just to keep afloat in a straight line, he smoothly stroked his board back and forth across the unbroken face, never once letting his rails out of the water. When the wave finally held up, enough to close out unimpressively on a sandbar covered with ignorant bathers, he coolly hooked himself into the tightest corner of the lip he could find, coiled his body and then stood crouching, poised to pounce as soon as the critical moment arrived. The faintest trace of energy washed through the wave face as the lip began to crumble and then, with an instinctive scoop upward, Hobgood elevated his board off the top, hoisting his tail skywards to lift into a seamless, three-foot-high, front-side air-three-sixty reverse.

Whatever we'd thought before went out the window. This kind of surfing *could* be done in Britain and the excitement that came with that revelation bubbled within me for the remaining two days of the contest.

By the time the normally cool-headed Rob Machado trudged up the sand, venting fury at the judging decision that had seen him come second overall to the Brazilian Renato Wanderley, our doors of perception had been blown wide open.

And then, just a short drive south to stay at Maureen and Pete's – family friends of the Groves – we were plonked back in what felt like the real world, eating tea and embellishing the stories together, ready to make our mates jealous when we got home the next day.

That is the bubble-like feeling that the Newquay microcosm can give you. It took us less than a day to start feeling as if the pros shredding on UK shores had just been a dream. The next morning Val drove us out west again to surf tiny Praa Sands, with a strong offshore wind and crystal clear but freezing water. We spent the session trying sluggishly to launch even the smallest of airs, before returning stiff-limbed to the beach to serenely accept our status as the humblest of surfing mortals.

Now, as the Truro sun warmed my black T-shirt, I remembered why, all those years ago, I hadn't been upset in any way by our pitiful attempt to impersonate the pros that morning. Back out into the wilds, beyond Truro, Falmouth, beyond even Helston, the striking, desolate beauty of Praa Sands had helped. Surrounded by rolling fields, its deep blue water washed around headlands of heightened summer greens, making the British coastline appear alive and invigorated by summer's warmth. Although we didn't know it at the time, Cornwall's enchanting aesthetics had worked their spell on me then.

'Reckon there'd be a wave at Praa Sands today?' I asked Rich, who had pulled his shades down and was lying on his back.

He didn't flinch. I thought he was asleep, but then he lethargically offered a response. 'Yeah, but it'd be a massive paddle – still tons of swell there today and a bit of wind. Won't be anything like you remember it.' I wondered if he'd been going through the same memory process as me. 'And anyway,' he continued. 'I've got to work tomorrow. Didn't you say you wanted to meet that mate of yours as well?'

By 'that mate of yours' he was referring to the 'shaper' Luke Young. A shaper is someone who makes surfboards by hand, and for years Luke had been making every board I ever used. Math's older brother had gone to uni with him, which was how we knew each other. Luke was doing pretty well for himself these days, but remained just as keen to make a good board for the friends who, by testing them out, had helped him learn the trade. He'd been promising for ages to roll out a red carpet if I ever turned up at his home break near Plymouth, and it had been in the back of my mind to see if Hurricane Bill might facilitate this.

Rich had a point – if he had to be home tomorrow then Plymouth was in the right direction, so I got out my phone and dialled Luke's number.

'Whassappenin', clart?' bellowed a voice after only a few rings. Luke loved to use the mock Newport accents he'd heard on Goldie Lookin' Chain tracks, having once been asked to make a couple of boards for the pseudo-rappers to use in a parody photoshoot. 'You oroi' or wha'?'

'Not bad, like, tidy! What're you up to?' A testament to Luke's impersonation skills lay in the fact that I, despite being only half an hour down the road from 'the 'port', couldn't use the lingo as adeptly as this Hertfordshire-born Plymouth transplant. 'I'm in Truro, like. Fancy a surf or wha'?'

'Oh, you're in Truro are you, spa? Safe, like!'

'So any waves in your neck of the woods, clart?'

He went quiet for a moment. 'You're really in Cornwall? No way!'

'Yeah, I'm really in Cornwall.' Was I this well known for being reluctant to head down here?

'Well, as it happens, spa, there is a bit of surf. I'm gonna check Chally out in about three hours' time. That gives you an hour and a half to leave Truro, if the traffic's OK.'

'An hour and a half? If there're waves your way, I'll leave now. What's it gonna be like?'

'It'll be smaller than where you are, but the sun's gonna be out – people are back in work after the weekend and there'll be some wedgy lefts.'

'Sounds great to me. I'll get driving, so we'll be on our way in five.'

'That'll leave you plenty of time. Safe!'

'Safe!'

I hung up and looked at Rich – for whom one side of the conversation had contained enough information. 'What d'you reckon then?'

'We've got time for the scenic route,' he said, stretching and standing up.

The scenic route, after a few sets of traffic lights, was the A390 to Liskeard, which first took us towards St Austell, passing through the Grampound area along the way. With the window down and one foot dangling in the air outside, Rich spent the first half-hour pointing to un-signposted turnings on our right and commenting, 'There's the sickest reef break down there,' or 'Me and my mate Stu checked this beachie down that road once and reckon in just the right swell there's gonna be a hell of a wedge off the headland.'

After St Austell, the road narrowed to one lane each way and began climbing and dropping through the parts of Cornwall that I'd never imagined taking delight in passing through. In the past I'd been far too insular in my approach to look out the window.

Great fir forests lined the flanks of rolling hills, broken only by the occasional spire or farmhouse. Some cool names began cropping up, every bit as novel as the ones you come across in Scotland. 'St Blazey' preceded 'Porcupine', 'Fairy Cross' and 'Taphouse' before dual-carriageways started again at 'Dobwalls'. For vast swathes of the journey, Cornwall looked sublimely desolate. Even the built-up areas appeared as old as the bedrock itself, with walls of thick, ancient masonry, thatch or slate roofs and knotted trees rising out of mossy-walled gardens.

By the time we crossed the Tamar Bridge and Plymouth started sprawling around us, I was, not for the first time on this trip, getting that feeling that events of the past few days had already slipped away into deepest memory. The stark contrast between lifestyles in the south-west has the ability to do that.

'Plymouth, man,' Rich moaned. 'In all the years I lived down here I always tried to avoid the place. Growin' up in Cardiff made me hate cities enough already.'

The Kingsbridge junction that Luke had told us about was east of the main city though, and immediately after taking it the rural serenity of the English countryside resumed. Another succession of quaint little villages rolled past our open windows, before a narrow lane bore a signpost for Challaborough. A few miles later, I started sensing sea air.

The road dipped repeatedly, each time around a bend that looked as though it would be the last before a beach appeared – until finally a thin lane led us down onto a small tarmaced ramp and a row of parking spaces. To our left was a pub and the entrance to a caravan park and out front a beach break. At the far end a set of cliffs rose from the reflective ocean surface, with a couple of quirkily designed homes sitting at the top and peering down over the swell lines that were moving in. Below these dream homes you could see that with a tiny bit more tide a left-hander would form, and beyond that was Bantham, the next bay over. Bantham was best known for the iconic Burgh Island and its famous hotel, which twice a day would get isolated by the sea washing in and cutting it off from the mainland. That event was due about now.

I sat on the wall overlooking the pebbly beach, watching the afternoon sun glint off the moving waves as their transient power moved towards the shoreline. A lone surfer was already in the water – a stocky goofyfooter (meaning he stood with his right foot forward). He had a zippy, agile style and was tearing in to the first few playful peaks of the incoming tide.

'Let's get in there, shall we?' I suggested to Rich.

'Shit yeah! Looks sweet.'

Slowly enough to enjoy the sun, but quick enough not to let too many more waves come through in our absence, we suited up, waxed our boards and stepped over a small stream that separated the car park from the surfing end of the bay.

Yesterday this beach would have been strewn with holidaymakers, but today only driftwood and a pair of dog-walkers were in evidence.

Here in South Devon the water was much colder than North Cornwall and I yelped as I set foot in it for the first time. But with the sun unblocked and still holding on to most of its summer strength, I'd recovered within a few paddles.

A pleasant surprise awaited us in the line-up. The goofyfoot we'd been watching was a mutual friend of mine and Luke's.

'Jonty!' I called out. He looked around and squinted for a moment, lifting his sandy-brown hair away from his dark forehead, his face burst in to a big white grin.

'Hey! What brings you down this way then, fella?' Sitting up on his board and treading water with his feet, he held a sun-tanned hand out. 'I haven't seen you for *ages*!'

I introduced him to Rich and explained where we'd been.

'Awesome. Road trip! Got to be done, eh? I love just getting in the car and driving, looking for waves. It's what it's all about.'

I agreed, and we set about exchanging a few waves as Challaborough's peak started to shift into place.

In such glassy conditions, and with only two others out, you could really relish being able to watch your wave grow and line itself up against the cliff. Given that we had no previous knowledge of the spot, it was helpful. You could judge and assess the way the sets refracted off the foot of the cliffs before rolling along the sandbar, and then moving through into a dumpy, seaweed-filled shore break.

After a few more waves, I spotted another surfer walking along the beach – a small guy with his wetsuit round his waist and head completely shaved. Although pretty distinctive anyway, this wasn't the main thing identifying the guy as Luke. He had a surfboard under his arm that sported some kind of punky, black and red spray job, each colour running over the other like blood, while a pink, chequered patch of pin-lined paint lingered underneath. He was renowned for this kind of artwork.

By the time he'd reached the edge of the water, he'd spotted us and punched the air as a greeting.

Typical Luke, he'd caught three waves before I even got to say hello to him face-to-face. Noted by friends for maintaining a permanent state of childlike stoke – a sort of constant grommet mentality, you could say – he kept spotting little waves on the inside and spinning around to catch them when he'd only paddled halfway out.

Eventually he made it in to the line-up, whereupon a quick high five was the only indicator that we didn't all surf together every day of the year. The four of us continued calling each other into waves, hooting each other's turns or snaps and talking about nothing in particular as we waited for the next set.

After a few days of thick right-handers, it was refreshing to surf on my backhand for such an extended period. The wave at 'Chally', as Luke and Jonty called it, was ideal for this as well. Its lip would hold up and break with forgiving timing, so each time you'd swung yourself around from the last turn it would be there again, wanting to connect with your board. You could build momentum easily as you rode across into a slightly slower section, which allowed you time to think before heading in to the shore break for a floater or a close-out re-entry.

In almost an hour of surfing the only other surfer to join us was a girl on a yellow board, bearing Luke's logo, who proceeded to shred a couple of waves herself. Luke had done some lecturing with her father up at the university, he explained, which was why she rode his boards.

'Don't need a reason,' said Jonty. 'Everyone rides his boards anyway. Luke owns this place!'

I asked what on earth a reprobate shaper and hardcore beach bum like Luke was doing lecturing, and he explained it was for the 'Surf Science' degree that was now being rolled out at Plymouth. How could I forget? This oddly titled course had become world famous. You could indeed now study surfing in uni.

'I go in as a guest shaper,' Luke explained proudly.

Rich, whose fins were cutting knife-like through the rear of the wave every time he came off the top, was having a ball. 'I never surf this side of the Tamar usually,' he pined, referring to what was effectively the border between Cornwall and Devon. 'I'll have to do it more often, man. What a vibe.'

'This is a great spot,' I said, looking up at the houses above us, with their great sheets of panoramic glass and landscaped gardens.

Rich agreed. 'I want to live in one of those pads, man. This place is wicked. Sweet waves, sun, it's completely cruisey.'

'Enjoy it while it's here,' said Jonty, arriving next to us in the line-up. 'I heard there's a front coming in tomorrow. It's gonna be the start of autumn again. But hey, perfect end-of-trip feel for you guys.'

He had a point. The thought of a day's rain once we'd made it back to Wales seemed strangely comforting. A chance to stay indoors and recover from days of constant surfing.

A wave swung into the bay then, bouncing off the cliff twenty yards ahead of us and swelling into a satisfying and tempting peak. With a splash, I dug in and paddled after it.

'My turn,' I grinned, poised, ready to go and looking down the line at a moment of suspended bliss.

Yes, there was something in what Jonty had said. This was a moment and nothing more, a sensation soon to be gone: this was the essence of a surf trip. As my hands gripped my rails, ready to push me to my feet, it occurred to me that this time I'd be sure to keep hold of these moments, to try and take them home with me. If indeed that was possible. Never again would I leave something so valuable behind on a trip to the south-west.

At the bottom of the wave, I dropped my back knee, felt for the face with my leading hand and waited for the right time to turn.

CHAPTER 9
THE RIVER SEVERN: BRITAIN'S LONGEST WAVE

The Severn Bore is a bit like Marmite. The main similarity is that as a surfer you'll either love it or you'll hate it. However, I must also say that the wave itself *is like Marmite*, in as much as it's brown, sticky, smelly, slimy, sludgy and – when you inevitably get face-planted somewhere and duly force-fed a load of its trademark filth – you'll discover it too has a very distinctive taste. And how could it not? There aren't many places in the world where you can ride naturally occurring waves dozens of miles upstream. Tidal bores are immensely different prospects to wind-created sea-waves, offering a challenge even to the most savvy of beach bums.

I had always really wanted to surf the bore, although like so many of my other bright British ideas, the convenience of Porthcawl and its surrounding spots had always stood in the way. When the bore was due to occur while I was in the country, I'd simply end up surfing somewhere else. Laziness could be blamed for some of it, but the other problem was that the bore happened on the biggest tides of the year – which in the case of the Bristol Channel meant it almost always coincided with great surf elsewhere. The power of half the ocean literally flowing towards the shore might send a two-foot wave gushing up the River Severn, but fifty miles further down the channel it would also lead to swell at rare high-tide river mouths and rocky outcrops; which meant that to score the bore you'd usually need to drive away from great waves. This is most certainly forbidden in the highest of surfing's commandments.

With this in mind, my ears still pricked up when I got a phone call on my way back from Cornwall. In traffic moving at about five miles an hour down the M5 after a crash up ahead, and with Rich sleeping in the passenger seat, my buzzing mobile caught my attention.

An offer to finally score one of the world's strangest waves was about to come my way. It was Breige, who had just been to see her friend Anne (with whom we'd bussed through Panama and Costa Rica a few years ago during the *Riding the Magic Carpet* journeys).

'Anne reckons the bore's gonna break in a few days' time – fancy going up? She can show us exactly where to get it. Oh, and *when* to get it as well. That's just as important.'

'Er...' It seemed odd to be arranging exact surf times for days ahead but, then again, this wasn't exactly going to be conventional surfing.

'Come on,' Breige insisted. 'There's no swell due for ages now. Where's Grovey, by the way?'

'Sleeping.'

'Cool. So he's not hearing this conversation then?'

'No.'

'Good. Don't tell him. Anne's only got room for you and me.' That's surfer loyalty for you.

'No worries. So do we need to go and see her first?'

'Well, we're going to meet on the prom for a coffee later if you're back in time.'

'She's in Porthcawl then?'

'Yeah. We should try and do this. You realise the bore usually breaks when its freezing – but this is a chance to actually surf it when the water's gonna be warm. And Anne always goes up there when it's breaking. She loves it. I reckon that's half the battle – being able to get to the right place and all that. But with her we'll be fine for all that.'

It was starting to sound more convincing.

'OK. I'll let you know how this traffic goes.'

Three hours later, with Rich safely dropped off, I was parking up on Porthcawl seafront for a 'business meeting' with Breige and Anne, who turned up with a tourist map of Gloucestershire.

'I know an OS map would be better,' she laughed, 'but you can still see the bends in the river with this thing.'

I looked across at the blueing, pond-flat seas out front. It was a sunny day in late season and the dog-walkers and retirees of the sleepy Welsh seaside were out in force. We got a couple of 99s and a coffee in before continuing to plan our surf in two days' time. I started taking stock of moments in this country when I thought its surfing experience was as far removed as possible from that of the rest of the world. *This* had to be one of the most bizarre to date, I decided.

'We can catch it in three places,' Anne explained, 'if we go to the north bank, that is – just beyond Chepstow. We'll end up in Gloucester either way, but I've wondered a few times now about trying to run around on the south bank. It's not going to have as many people on it. The bore gets crowded, you see.'

'Does that matter?' I asked.

'Well, not as much as the shape of the riverbank does. Maybe I'll have a look on Google Earth tonight. We need to avoid big sandbanks or obstacles, see. If you hit something while riding the bore, trust me, you'll really know about it. There's a *lot* of power in that water. Our main problem, whatever standard of surfer you are, is gonna be catching it and getting to your feet. It's pot luck. You'll see what I mean when you paddle for it.'

It was with nerves not really experienced since competing as a youngster that I tried to sleep two nights later, knowing that tomorrow, after decades of hearing about it, I was going to ride the Severn Bore. At about ten, just as I was winding down, Anne had texted with some last-minute info:

Got better map. Upper Framilode, Longney and Elmore seem best placed on the south bank. Will see you guys at seven – we can sort it out then. Anne

This didn't help. I was really struggling to imagine what awaited me in the morning: a wall of violent, surging water running through unfamiliar land. A place where surfers were nobodies; the English countryside.

A few perturbed hours of half-sleep later, the alarm went off.

It was as clear a morning as the Severn Estuary region could present. Perhaps to make up for some of the raging oceans and Atlantic tempers, on a crisp autumn morning the whole stretch does have the ability to appear as sleepy as if it were encased in a glass snowstorm. On a tide of this size, though, that's a deceiving impression. Behind the veneer of stillness, a force was building that would command our respect.

The Severn Bore occurs as a result of a massive build-up of sea water in the Bristol Channel, which reaches a critical point and then haemorrhages into the River Severn. It occurs hundreds of times a year but breaks big enough to ride on about ten or twenty of those occasions. The expanse of water from Cardiff to Chepstow, over which the Severn Bridge eventually crosses, acts as a funnel for the water that gets forced up it by the biggest full-moon tides of the year. At the top of the channel billions of gallons of water are crammed into an increasingly smaller estuary, where they meet the oncoming downstream flow of the river. Here a massive, swelling, stand-off of water occurs. Since so much weight and energy can only be held in place for a short time, something has to give – and at the very top of the tide it does, in the form of what is quite literally a tidal wave – the sea effectively flash-floods the river, with the subsequent surge pouring upstream for hours.

The bore stops at nothing, has no 'back' (unlike an ocean wave) and is propelled by the weight of an entire sea. And, since it breaks for hours and miles, it can also be *surfed* for hours and miles. From conception to its final dissipation at a weir just beyond Gloucester, it lasts over thirty miles, in fact, although to date the record for riding it lay at somewhere between five and seven miles – depending on who you asked.

On an empty M4 motorway, we passed the city of Newport lit with the oranges of a rising, autumnal sun. Buildings glistened, a smoke stack rose straight up untouched by wind, and beyond that the sea could be seen, swelling with the fullness of an enormous ego. The moon's magnetic pull had given it the power to encroach further than its usual entitlement. As the road bridged over the River Isca, which was testing its banks to their very limit, I looked back at the Newport skyline and was reminded of the ominous calm of Wordsworth's famous observations on Westminster Bridge: *The beauty of the morning; silent, bare…* and then this:

Ne'er saw I, never felt, a calm so deep!
The river glideth at his own sweet will:
Dear God! the very houses seem asleep;
And all that mighty heart is lying still!

In just over an hour the River Severn would be doing anything but lying still.

That said, there is still an element of the farcical to the whole Severn Bore rigmarole. I defy anyone not to pull up in a car park in the English countryside, suit up and then begin waxing your board next to a smoothly flowing river without feeling like a complete prat. Granted, we weren't the only ones, but my self-consciousness was at an all-time high as I tucked my dad's big blue longboard (sneakily borrowed without his knowledge in the early hours, in keeping with a lifelong tradition) under my arm and began searching for a way down the riverbank.

There was a lot about this that I wasn't used to: crawling through stinging nettles and thorn bushes to get to the water's edge for one. Beyond that there was the mud and the texture of the river. As I dallied at the top of the bank, another surfer, perfectly equipped with life jacket and an old pair of trainers, pushed me aside and demonstrated how to get into the River Severn – by sliding down a slope of mud and sludge on his arse, board held neatly in the air. With a plop, the landlocked local had made me look like a sissy. Anne and Breige promptly followed him, after which it was my turn.

Lucky not to ding my dad's board, I made it to the fresh water, only to discover that the lower density (due to no saline content) made even a longboard lose a lot of buoyancy. I'd heard many times before that the biggest board you could find was needed to approach the bore, and was quickly beginning to see why.

'This is getting better by the minute,' said Breige as we started to paddle out into the middle of the wide section of river.

'Yeah. And weirder,' I replied.

A few hundred yards downstream there was a big sandbank on the opposite side of the river. With the bore not due for another ten minutes we 'beached' ourselves on it, sat down and began to wait.

This gave me another chance to have a good look around at where exactly this mad foray into British surfing had now put me. Lining the banks on one side was the village of Newnham. Sloping its way to the river's edge, it seemed a lazy place – a classic, quaint English village, which probably had summer fetes and farmers' markets. A stone wall and quayside protected a large pub from the water a little upstream and beyond that was a stretch of mudflats and then naught but countryside. I spotted a gap in the banks that I fancied trying to ride up to, as it would allow a nice simple exit from the water. Trying to scale the stone wall in the rushing wake of a bore didn't look like fun at all. Putting the longboard on one edge in the sand and sludge, I sat on the other.

'Is this it then?' I asked Anne, the only one of our party who had been here before.

'Yeah,' she said. 'This is it. Now we just wait. Sometimes it's early, sometimes late. We'll be able to see it way off though, so I reckon we just wade back into the river when it comes around that corner.'

'That corner' was a turn about a mile downstream, in the nape of which was a large rusting boat. It looked as though the river separated hilly Wales on one side from flat Gloucestershire on the south. From among what must have been farmland I could see a few cars parked up, way downstream, and out of the grasslands a couple of other surfers were wandering dutifully to the river's edge.

'They'll never make it all the way to us, will they?' I asked Anne.

'Probably not. And if they do then this sandbank will probably get them. Remember: don't get stuck behind any obstacles.'

'Right, thanks.'

With only a few minutes left before the supposed arrival time, three more prospective bore riders made their way into the river. Two set up on the other side to us – the same bank as our car – while the other appeared on a kayak from way upstream. Life-jacketed up neatly, he greeted us, smiling.

'Good spot there, guys. You'll get on OK from that point.'

He seemed to be in the know and immediately we tried to quiz him further. Unlike locals anywhere else in the surfing world, he was completely content to tell us everything he could. We learned that 'she' had been arriving five minutes late this week, but that the riverbed had been allowing for good power. Apparently we were also lucky to have picked what so far seemed not to be a particularly busy day (although almost a hundred spectators were now lining the stone wall in anticipation). My favourite little tip was that the wave could be ridden three miles from here without difficulty.

'The wife's in Longney,' he added. 'She's got the car there, see. I'm gonna get the wave to there and then move on to Overbridge. Are you gonna go there too? It's the last place to catch it before the weir. If you do go to Overbridge, paddle into her *after* she's passed through the bridge with the pilings because the river bed always goes deep on the way under – stops feeling the bottom. You'll lose her if you're up and riding before then. The foundations have made trenches along the bottom. Catch her after the bridge.'

We all thanked him and got into position, which involved wading about five yards into the river and waiting – anxiously, I might add.

'I can't believe how nervous I am about a two-foot wave,' Breige admitted. I had butterflies too. What if I couldn't catch it? Or what if I fell off straight away? The immense power and scale of the water behind this wave was right there at the front of my mind too. In Porthcawl you had utmost reverence for the tide, which was deadly during these full-moon spells. People got swept to sea at high water, sometimes never to be seen again, while at low tide shipwrecks from centuries ago reappeared, eerie and skeletal. Here in the wide, rolling River Severn, the waiting time added to the aura and mystery of the impending bore.

It was as much a relief as it was a rush when, moments later, what looked like a small crease in the surface rounded the corner in the distance.

'That's it!' the canoeist hooted. 'That is it!'

I squinted, trying to make out what was happening to the water downstream. A dark ripple was moving sternly forward, with clearly defined patches of broken white appearing here and there, either spreading or slackening off depending on what the river was doing. For one moment it would appear almost unnoticeable, before seconds later breaking quickly across the entire expanse of the river. This process rolled over and over a few times, with the size and scale becoming more discernable as it neared.

The canoeist, meanwhile, continued amping. 'Ooh – she's a beauty today,' he said, as white water exploded against the hull of the derelict boat. In the middle distance I made out some of the first row of surfers now up and riding, but by the time the shape of the Severn Bore was really making itself known to us they were all off and wading back to their cars. It didn't look as if anyone had held on for long at all.

It seemed an age yet before the river started violently pulling towards the approaching wave and I realised it was time to start going through the motions. Way bigger than the wave had seemed at first, it was with some adrenaline that I started paddling and felt the wall of water slam into me. With no need to hurry, I lay prone on the board and waited for the sensation to settle. We were riding a tidal bore.

Lying down was enough for the first minute or so; none of us made any attempt to stand up as we waited for the right section. The canoeist kept directing us out into the middle, or back to the bank, as the wave changed shape. He did indeed seem to know exactly what he was doing.

'Right – we can spread out now,' he said. 'She's showing the whole way across for a little while from here.'

At that, I popped up, only to wobble hideously as I remembered the weaker density of the water beneath me. The deep, single fin of my dad's longboard was slipping away and I had to really work to balance my weight out enough. The fin needed to be driven, but if I put too much weight too far back then the wave would start to outrun me.

During the first stage of the ride, I'd really enjoyed taking in my surroundings and laughing to Breige and Anne as we lay like total beginners on our massive boards. But now on my feet I could concentrate only on what I was doing and nothing else. My board's rails were pinching desperately to the river's surface, reacting completely differently to how they would on an ocean wave. The constant nature of the powerful bore was your best friend and worst enemy. There was no ebb and flow to it – whatever the wave did, wherever it went, the rhythm and speed were the same. The entire River Severn was moving forward with clockwork inevitability.

Gradually, I began to communicate with it. There was no need to worry about climbing or dropping for speed – the wall would keep you going whatever – so I started trying to arc out into the middle, to the shoulder of the wave, turning back in again a few times with increasing force. Meanwhile, the only other person I was aware of was the canoeist, still there, still riding and calling instructions to me – which I could no longer hear over the sound of rushing water.

After several of these half-attempts at cutting back, I felt the wave's hold on the riverbed start to slacken. It was hitting an underwater trough. Angling back for the bank, I tried to get across it before it stranded me. Within seconds things had changed, though, and I was too late. I could see my board losing the race and the Severn Bore slipping mercilessly underneath me, carrying Breige, Anne and the canoeist on towards the bend ahead.

I didn't care, though. It had been great, and now behind the wave I was able to really see its power and force. The island of sand on which we'd waited was now nowhere to be seen, but rather just a churning mass of angry brown sea, surging upstream.

As if unaware of how it got here and now afraid, trapped, confused as to its whereabouts, the ocean water behind the bore looked erratic and unpredictable. And I was floating in its midst.

Now was the time to act quickly. You had to be bullish in your methods to get back up the riverbank and onto dry land; any delays would see you dragged yet further upstream. Anne's car was already way behind us by the time I'd climbed through the bushes and mud to find the road. Filthy, but laughing to myself, I wandered back and waited for the other two, who arrived a couple of minutes later, also covered in mud.

'Sorry Anne. How are we gonna get these muddy wetsuits home?'

'Don't worry about that. I've got some tarp in the boot to sit on. Quickly, let's get the boards inside and head after it! Come on, it'll be at Minsterworth in half an hour.'

She opened the boot of her Mondeo Estate and started forcing my dad's now mud-caked longboard across the passenger seat. Breige's followed, before we ourselves were crammed like cargo into the space that was left. Anne then shoved her own board, borrowed from the Llangennith surf school in which she worked, over our heads, and the chase was on.

You can catch the Severn Bore in several different spots. We had foregone ideas of the south bank this morning, because the easiest way to get three attempts in was to stick to the route Anne knew well. As bore virgins, we'd wanted to get the best chance possible of scoring a ride. Now that we'd done that, all that remained was to enjoy the rest of the craziest morning of surfing available on British shores (if in fact a flood plain in the middle of the English countryside can count as a shore).

The next parking spot was next to the most famous pub on the stretch, the Severn Bore Inn, which, given that it was one of the very few buildings along this part of the bank, probably owed the lion's share of its business to an ingenious piece of naming. St George bunting was billowing in what was now a light morning breeze – the day was finally drawing breath and coming to life. Outside the pub were signs, crudely handwritten and alerting spectators to the fact that the world-famous bore could be seen here this morning at 9 a.m.

Taking a little lane along the pub's right flank, we had to push through a crowd that had spilled out from the beer garden. They soon parted once they smelled us coming – none of them wanting to get any of our mud on themselves. The river was a welcome chance to rinse some of the dirt off. We were soon all three side by side, paddling slowly back downstream away from the onlookers and around the bend in the river, where total serenity awaited. A basking heron glanced at us, uninterested as we sat and waited in waist-deep water.

For almost a quarter of an hour the only sounds anywhere were the birds calling around us, the trees swaying softly and the river gently eddying towards what it thought was a smooth entry to the sea. I glanced at my watch. 'She' was again running late.

The first sound that appeared out of the ordinary was that of a bush stirring on the other side – before a voice called out 'Woahh!' and a surfer plopped sideways into the water from among the foliage. His board followed half a second behind and cracked him neatly on the head – a moment of slapstick that Laurel and Hardy would have been proud of. He looked up, dazed, and then called over to us. 'Am I in the right place?'

'I dunno,' I replied. 'We don't know what we're doing.'

'Oh,' he sighed to himself – looking almost relived. 'That's OK, then.'

He started paddling across to us, when a speedboat suddenly rounded the corner ahead and tore past us. It was carrying a family in puffed orange life jackets. I waved at them and one of the kids shouted out, 'It's coming!'

There was just enough time for the boat's irritating wake to wash around us and lap the edges of the river before the bore swirled into view again. It was now much bigger than it had been earlier, but moving at that same steady yet formidable pace. All four of us started trying to guess where to get onto it. Twenty yards away it looked to be backing off a little, before at about ten feet off it abruptly peeled halfway across the river, pitching forward in a way that would have certainly allowed an agile and already riding surfer to pull into a quick tube. The white water again hit us with a thump, and when the initial shock settled I looked around to see that all four of us were successfully cruising the river while lying on our stomachs.

From there I started thinking about jumping to my feet earlier than last time, but then I felt a change in the water depth under me and thought it best to lie down for a little longer. This turned out to be unequivocally the worst decision of the day so far, as one of the heaviest wipeouts of my life was now seconds away.

On most other occasions, in my surfing experiences to date, I have always known, or at least been vaguely aware of, when a terrible wipeout could be about to happen. That's a good thing, as it means you're prepared for it and are less likely to get hurt – and in fact less likely to come off in the first place. Lying prone and riding a waist-high Severn Bore, though, you are not thinking about life and limb. But you should be, as I learned approaching the bend ahead when I suddenly saw the riverbed beneath me drain itself dry – allowing me a lovely ramp of rock and mud to run aground on.

There are beatings, and then there are beatings. Mind you, I wouldn't even call what happened next a beating. I'd call it a flogging – no a wracking, or even a hanging, drawing and quartering, a crucifixion. Bouncing across the bottom I was already bruising when the roots of a tree, half ripped out and completely obstructing any further passage, emerged in front of me. Without time to think of anything, I was stopped dead – hitting it with a thud that made my neck crick loudly above the roar of moving water shredding the riverbanks. A person then bashed into me under the surface – Anne, as I later found out – before being carried on and leaving me stuck face-first against a lump of soil, rock and root.

Again my ocean instincts served only to get me into further trouble. When a 'normal' wave smashes you into something it promptly recedes, allowing a chance to free yourself. That's because ocean swells have both a front and back – a rise and fall in water level. The Severn Bore, however, has no such back – remember it's a tidal surge – like a mini-tsunami. Once it has passed, the water behind it is two-feet deeper and will continue to push for miles. This is why these sorts of waves are so incredibly destructive. It's not the initial impact – although considerable in itself – that does the damage. The bulk of the danger comes from the unstoppable heap of water behind. If you've ever tried to carry a full bucket of water, you'll recall the weight of water easily. This, though, was several trillion buckets – it was like having all the swimming pools in Britain poured over you.

It wasn't long before I realised my predicament and then fear kicked in. If I couldn't prise myself free then I would drown and, of all the places I'd been and waves I'd surfed, my posthumous ego wouldn't have coped well with that happening thirty miles inland between Newnham and Gloucester. The taste of mud was trying its best to overwhelm me as I started trying to push sideways. Something else then smacked into me – a tree stump as it happened – and I was torn out from the obstacle ahead, careering and somersaulting underwater but crucially flowing freely upstream again.

When I emerged, spluttering and choking, it was to the sound of people applauding and laughing from the beer garden of the Severn Bore Inn. Each of them were showered and dressed in comfy clothes, looking as punchable as any human I'd yet laid eyes on. I wanted to shout 'You try it, ya bastards', before common sense got the better of me and I remembered to worry about Breige and Anne, who had also both been slammed at roughly the same spot. How would I explain such irresponsible behaviour to Breige's father if we returned to Wales with his daughter gravely wounded by a tidal wave?

Fortunately I didn't have to worry long, because only a few yards ahead I spotted that she and Anne had been treated much more leniently in their wipeouts, allowing them a good chance to also laugh at my near-death experience. I knew that most surfing mates would be obliged to enjoy your misfortune – but your girlfriend? Well, you learn something new about surfers all the time.

Expecting a hero's welcome back on land again, I was yet further exasperated to see that the public gallery, rather than wanting to make a fuss of me and mill around praising my no-guts-no-glory approach, were all racing back to their cars to try and watch the bore again at its last easy-access point, where the A48 bridged back over the river and into the city of Gloucester.

This, surely, was going to be where all three of us would score the ride of the day. In a perfect world, maybe. The Severn Bore, however, is many things – but perfect is not one of them.

Although who would want it to be? It's the sheer quirkiness of pulling up in places like the half-finished Redrow Estate we parked in next that makes the whole escapade what it is. At the third take-off spot we walked down a small lane, stepping gingerly around clusters of dog poo, and negotiating a little side cesspool of shopping trolleys and floating litter to wade out into the river for our final rendezvous with what we were hoping would now be the most powerful section of the bore.

The words of the canoeist – who was probably smugly back with 'the wife' after his three-mile ride – were in my mind. Catch it after the pilings, because the water was deep around the foundations. There were three bridges in a row, though, so I began looking for pilings that had been driven directly into the riverbed. It looked most likely to be the first of the structures. The A48 crossing over the Severn was by far the biggest piece of construction work but it didn't touch the riverbed, which actually seemed pretty shallow there. I set myself up right underneath it, with the sound of cars rolling by overhead. Breige and Anne moved a little further upstream and sat about twenty yards away. It would have been a tranquil little moment if a Scottish guy on a bodyboard hadn't emerged from the other side of the road and slipped under the bridge to sit by me.

'All right!' he grinned. 'Always wanted to try surfin', like! Couldn't miss this for the world.'

Realising how silly I looked by taking this at all seriously, I asked him where he'd found the board.

'Borrowed it off a mate. Reckon it'll be OK?'

I couldn't really think of an answer to that. A longboard would barely hook onto the bore properly, so a bodyboard without flippers wasn't much different to having no board at all.

'I don't know, man,' I said. 'I haven't a clue what I'm doing.' For the second time today this was a great ice-breaker. He laughed, congratulated me and wondered aloud what to do when the bore came.

Treading water, the guy was soon carried downstream – and barring a miracle I knew he wouldn't be coming back this way on the face of a wave. But he'd probably have a story to tell later, which was sure to be worth his while.

The first indication of this third encounter with the bore was the crowd up on the banks above us drawing breath loudly. I could see why when a solid wall of dark wet menace rounded the corner and feathered just before the first bridge – before breaking directly in front of it with a series of explosions. Against my expectations it was breaking through the pilings, which could well mean I'd chosen the wrong spot...

Heart beating and out of breath with excitement, I turned upstream and started paddling desperately. Behind me I could hear the wave sucking away at the land around it. I took a look over my shoulder and saw it speeding towards me. Only a few yards away it was still there and steep enough to catch – until the moment it arrived under the bridge I had waited by. Here, as if someone had turned a switch, it suddenly disappeared, sneaking under and onwards. Whatever I did was hopeless – yes, it *was* the bridge the canoeist had referred to. I groaned as my chance slipped away. I wondered how many of the spectators at this place had also seen my humiliation at Minsterworth a short while ago. It had to be the vast majority of them for sure.

To make things worse, only a few paces further on, the wave rose back up and the last thing I saw, before realising that I quickly needed to get out of here, was Breige and Anne jumping up and riding smugly away into the distance.

Having one chance and one chance only to catch a wave that you've waited fifteen minutes for is completely alien to most surfers, for whom the general frolic of trying to catch hordes of waves in one session is part of the pleasure of the sport. That feeling of being active and dashing around the sea in circles, chasing wave after wave, is often synonymous with the height of surf stoke. But something has to be said for the crescendo of anticipation that comes from standing in flat water and waiting on a one-off opportunity. It's got more of the mystical element to it – like the 'fifty-year storm' that

Point Break's makers so infuriatingly invented in that famous scene when Bodhi is beatified by giving his life to the one wave that he had always dreamed of. Here, though, in the heart of Gloucestershire, that same idea was very much a reality – a wave that felt like an entity to be sought out or hunted down.

And its followers were a different tribe altogether; a bunch of beings innocent in their knowledge of the fashions and codes of surfing as I knew it and free of the bullshit that it came with – but with just the same dedication and desire to break away from the crowd.

It was a good twenty minutes before the girls found their way back to the car, which I spent sitting at the curbside feeling the light warmth of the autumn sun on my wetsuit and chatting to a pair of long-haired bore enthusiasts, who were changing in the Transit van next to me.

'Hey – you were one of the ones that stood up back at Newnham, weren't you?' one of them said to me. 'Respect, man! That's hard core. You should get a bigger board – then you might get a few miles on it. On your feet, like.'

'Yeah, maybe,' I nodded. 'I'm not sure boards do get much bigger than this, mind.'

'I dunno. If you go down to the coasts they might. I've heard about these things that they stand on like – *as* they paddle them. Crazy that, eh? Saw it on a video, man.'

He meant the stand-up paddle craze that was driving people in Porthcawl mad – involving boards that were sometimes twice the size of the one I'd ridden today. These crafts were so oversized that riders could stand on them and move through the water with a kayak-style paddle. 'Yeah – I've seen those things too,' I nodded.

He put his keys in the ignition and then called over to me: 'Anyway, mate, we're off for lunch. Severn Bore Inn, if you wanna swing by on the way back. Might see you there. Nice to meet you, man.'

As their aged van turned noisily on Redrow's fresh tarmac, belching a quick dose of exhaust fumes in my direction, I was left dwelling on one thing from the conversation I'd just had.

Down the coasts, he had said – as if it were a place nobody had ever been to – least of all me. Britain, I realised for the first time in my life, had a surf scene that never went to the beach. It was strangely humbling.

That afternoon I paddled out in windy Rest Bay, mainly to wash the mud out of my wetsuit and to check that my body could still get across an ocean wave with all these bruises. The swell was laced with a bit of autumn juice and the usual crew of familiar faces were out and riding – moaning about the shape of waves, the speed of the tide, water temperature, weather fronts. Whatever they could think of to trivialise what was, to them, just another meaningless go-out in a lifetime of addiction to the sea and all its moods.

Of course, I can't deny being as underwhelmed as the rest of them. This session was nothing out of the ordinary and I'd suffered nowhere near enough wave-deprivation lately to appreciate this for anything more than the light exercise it provided. But there was something in me that was relishing every wave, feeling every inch of every turn. My perceptions of what surfing was in the UK and what it meant, although already undergoing a huge metamorphosis, had changed more in this one day than any other I could recall.

'Tides are getting smaller soon. Can't wait,' one of the groms was promising his younger brother. 'Waves'll get easier to surf again then.'

He had a point, but with those smaller tides the bore would also shrink, hidden from both view and memory for the next stage of the lunar cycle. The ocean would always be there to satisfy an appetite for surf – but I knew already that the next time the bore was expected to break there was a strong chance I'd again be dashing east across the M4 at dawn – *away* from the sea – to that ludicrous wait for a bucking, twisting wave that, although borne of the sea, had broken free from its rules and rhythms. On the wildest tides of the year, the Severn Bore exists as a quick display of dissent or escapism for the ocean-minded. It's a cheeky bit of infidelity, as well as a solid reminder of what surfing is ultimately all about: the wait, the chase – and then, as I had been learning of late, nothing but the moment.

CHAPTER 10
FIRST BROKEN BOARD

orthcawl Point's most experienced and hardened locals can be distinguished from the rest of the flock by one characteristic: they *jump* out rather than paddle out.

This is often the case in point breaks. There will be a set of little-known rocks that allow easy entry into the line-up without needing to paddle from the beach – which is by far the safest route. You can get out to Porthcawl Point – which is, as the crow flies, the closest surf spot to my house – from either Coney Beach or Trecco Bay each side of it. It takes ages, and this is really frustrating as on a good day it means having to watch set after set of great surf break on the horizon, while all you can do is puff and pant against a rip. The line-up gets closer at a patience-sapping slow rate, and if you're at all out of practice, you usually need a breather once you do make it.

But, throughout the decorated history of the spot, the toughened locals, the cream of the crop, the ones who run the show on crowded days, have known about and used another method.

Apart from one of them: yours truly.

The 'keyhole', or 'jump rock', was, I think, deemed out of bounds or off-limits to Andersons by some higher power.

My grandfather, John Anderson MBE, one of the most renowned swimming teachers ever to grace the beaches of South Wales, famously got in to trouble there about fifty years ago. My father Paul, a champion surfer in his day, had an experience on those rocks that he won't even talk about, and as a result will always leave the house twenty minutes early for a Point session, so that he can have time to paddle from one of the beaches. And then there's my brush with the place. It's not an exaggeration when I say that, to this day, my run-in with Porthcawl Point's keyhole as a sixteen-year-old is indeed the closest I have yet been to death. In fact, it's the closest I ever plan to come to death until the Reaper himself arrives with an irrevocable warrant from up on high.

And to put off the signing of that warrant, I am proud to be one of the only Porthcawl Point regulars who *never*, *ever*, in any circumstances, jumps off the rocks.

Again, like so many of my lesser moments in surfing, the ordeal I suffered that day was inextricably linked to the Welsh Nationals.

As a grommet, I belonged to an age group that had both good and bad luck on our side. The Junior European Surf Championships were held every two years – on the even-numbered years, as it happened – in a different location around the continent. This meant that, being born in one myself, I was always amongst the oldest in my category during the crucial years. Eligibility ran from 1 January, so I could compete in the 'youth' (under fourteen) at the maximum age of fourteen, 'cadets' (under sixteen) at the age of sixteen and then juniors while being eighteen on paper. It meant I had much more chance of making the national team than the half of my mates born before January. That bit was the good luck.

But this meant nothing to my mother. She was a teacher, and to her biennial consternation, it also meant that the most important surfing competitions of my life fell right smack in the middle of first GCSE and then A Level seasons. That can indeed be the undoing of many a grommet – Rich for one, who won the cadets category the day before his maths exam, and reckoned he couldn't concentrate on the sums in front of him for more than ten seconds.

He was lucky; his mum, Val, used to let him train and surf as much as he wanted. My villainous mother was nowhere near as accommodating and, with my dad nodding vaguely behind her, had drawn up a structured revision and surfing timetable with an incentive scheme at the end of it.

It was torture. I was allowed an hour of surfing a day on a weeknight and two a day on weekends – nowhere near enough to try and make it to the contest of a lifetime in Portugal later in the year – which you could only qualify for with a placing in the top two in your category at the Welsh.

She appointed my dad to work out a reward for getting the right grades. I'd been paying him in instalments for my favourite surfboard and he decided, in classic parental generosity, to make this the bargaining tool.

'If you get the grades your mother's decided you're capable of then I'll waive the rest of the surfboard debt,' he announced proudly.

'Great,' I replied, rolling my eyes.

I was, however, a step ahead of them. By coasting in school, I'd managed to con my mother into setting slightly lower ambitions than she may have otherwise had. As a result, while feigning pulling my hair out at the seeming impossibility of her targets, I was able to relax a little, knowing that both the free board *and* the Europeans berth were well within my reach – as long as I could get in the water enough. But that remained the hardest part to pull off.

There was, of course, one time of day when I could surf as much as I wanted. This was during school hours, when my parents were both at work. On the most important swells I would wander out of the gate at lunch or break times, whereupon the only challenge became concealing that my wetsuit was soaking when mum came home.

As it happened, the day before the Welsh Nationals presented one of the best swells in months. Study leave hadn't yet begun but, keen to make full use of the last-minute practice opportunity, I duly faked leaving for school only to turn around again and come home once I knew there was nobody at home. My part-owned surfboard was waxed up ready and, with my spring suit around my waist, I ran the few hundred yards towards the Point, which was breaking well overhead, with an offshore wind grooming its sets into fiercely hollow, thundering sections.

Thinking the universe was mine, I hopped along the sharp prongs of rock that indicated the route to the jump rock and keyhole, worked through a few quick and largely ineffective stretches and warm-ups, strapped on my leash and prepared to leap.

I'd never encountered any difficulty with the jump rock, after following one of the senior locals out one day. But then again I'd never tried to use it in a solid six-foot swell. The usual markers weren't there: the little spike of sea-worn bedrock that was supposed to submerge beneath the incoming wave when it was time to jump, the gulley that dragged you out into the deep patch behind, almost catapulting you into the line-up with the receding water.

Today, the whole launch pad was just awash with foamy, angry sea. Each incoming wave would slap loudly against the rows of jagged reef that marked the start of the Point. Seemingly miles behind me, I took a second look back at the beaches and wondered, only for a moment, whether it wouldn't be wiser to walk back and do it the safer way. That moment was enough for doubt to set in – and as soon as my feet left solid ground I knew it had all gone horribly wrong.

I landed in water, but had chosen a wave much smaller than the one that had broken before it. This meant that the wave had run into shallower water than usual and was about to suck back too quickly.

Sensing that I was in trouble, I kicked frantically with my feet and stroked desperately forwards, at this point still believing I could make it. I had to believe it. The alternative was horrendous.

As my board's fins caught rock below me, a million thoughts raced through my mind. I remembered another Porthcawl surfer, Anthony Cross, who had once had such a kicking here that for a moment his feet were sticking vertically up in the air with his head wedged between two ledges of sharp reef. Crossy's battering was captured on film and shown in surf club one night. I also remembered the times I'd personally seen people get crucified here. I'd usually enjoyed watching that from the comfort of the line-up, laughing and enjoying their misfortune.

The wave had now drained all remaining water from under me and I was left lying on my board with rock below me, rock in front of me and rock on both sides. The keyhole is a passageway between two much higher ledges that were now boxing me in, holding me in just the right place to get mercilessly smashed by the next oncoming wave – which was two or three times the size of the one I'd tried to jump.

As it hit me, survival instinct kicked in. Nothing else would matter as long as my head didn't smack anything. I heard the fibreglass of my board splintering as the wall of water made impact. That gushing, liberated water; a wave finally releasing its energy after thousands of miles at sea. It rolled me over and pinned me to the rock behind. Recognising it as a part of the shelf that seldom went underwater, I gripped on and tried to cling to it as the wave receded. Just as the bulk of it had drained away I lost hold though, sliding on my back across the ravine until my board, now wedged across the gap in front, broke my fall. I had a few seconds in which to take a breath and regain my balance, before the next one hit. This time it held my board back against me and flung me from the keyhole onto another slab of sharp rock. I was now marooned, hopelessly nowhere near either of the safe points. Unable to reach either the keyhole or the line-up behind (where I'd be able to tread water); all that was left to do was shriek.

The lifeguards stationed at the edge of Coney Beach, meanwhile, would have heard only half of that shriek as another wall of water slammed the air from my lungs.

This was now a very serious situation; realising drowning could be as little as one mistimed inhalation away. For some ten or twelve waves in a row, all I could do was get pulled across the rocks and then thrown back up them. All the while my board remained strapped to my right leg, weighing me down. Usually in this event you're supposed to release it, but I was never free enough to reach my foot. There were simply too many forces acting against me. How I escaped serious injury remains a mystery.

When I did eventually find myself back on dry land, it was only because the ocean had done with me. For reasons unknown, a sudden sideways surge had deposited me back at the keyhole, just as the sets held off for thirty seconds. It was as if the sea had decided enough was enough – as if it had taken pity on me, or at the very least grown bored of tormenting me.

Realising this could well be my only chance, I drew on every ounce of strength left in my body to climb back out of the gulley I had jumped into about a minute ago. Seeing the ground beneath take on the lighter grey hue of a rock yet to be wetted, I realised it was over. Almost.

My board was still attached to my leg, about to pull me back in.

In one last burst of panic, I began reeling my leash in like a fishing line. For something supposed to have a six-foot surfboard on the other end it wasn't offering a lot of resistance.

When I saw why, it was the final straw. At the end of my leash were the last few inches of my board, and nothing more. About half the tail was left – the rear fin and one side fin.

Not only was my board broken, but my spirit was too. As I surveyed no less than four separate pieces of unpaid-for surfboard floating in the hell below, I burst into tears.

And then another thought, also of pure survival, kicked in. *What the fuck was I going to tell my dad?*

Bleeding, with a torn wetsuit and eight inches of surfboard, I trudged across the rocks back to the grassy part of the point where the two lifeguards were standing, arms folded, having elected not to try and help me. It had been far more amusing to watch.

Like a typical teenage brat, I started yelling at them.

'What the fuckin' hell are you doing? I almost died. I *almost died*!'

This was when they started laughing.

In the years that followed, though, I realised the importance of this kind of disdain towards grommets. I deserved the embarrassment and ridicule that came with the fallout from that dreadful morning – in the long run it probably did me good. They say what doesn't kill you can only make you stronger – well surely that would apply here.

Of course, since they knew I was skiving school, the lifeguards were well aware of the pact that I had no option but to enter. If I didn't accept their banter – which went on to be pretty cutting – then they could always take things seriously and ring my parents.

Later that afternoon, I thought briefly that they had chosen to take it seriously. I walked in to Black Rock Surf Shop to ask the advice of Herbi, one of the godfathers of Welsh surfing. He tutted and expressed his sympathy, before showing me an 'incident report' that had arrived through his fax machine from Coney Beach lifeguard station.

'Oh, so they do recognise it as an "incident" now, eh?' I spat.

Herbi just grinned, blew a smoke ring, and handed me the thin piece of paper.

INCIDENT REPORT

Date: 5th May 1996   Location: Black Rocks/The Point

DETAILS: At the above mentioned time a cocky little grom, obviously fancying his chances of being THE MAN in one of the biggest swells of the year arrived at the Point. Thinking he was some kind of Hawaiian hellman, the dull twat decided to jump off the rocks when the surf was obviously not right for it. Pros have used the beach instead in swells like this, but undeterred the grommet made his way to the edge of the water with gay abandon.

Realising the little knobhead was gonna get his arse handed to him, the senior lifeguard on duty instructed us to watch from a safe distance. Apparently the grommet's grandfather 'would approve', so we positioned ourselves in good viewing distance, and prepared for the best entertainment of the year, since the pissed tramp tried to take his girlfriend swimming last August.

It was every bit as funny as we'd hoped. The grom got a proper turning, thoroughly deserved, and, best of all, began crying loudly for his mum.

Realising this was for his own good, we left him to it, and began taking bets on how many waves he'd get held down for. Psycho won with thirteen. An unlucky number for some but not least the grommet, who was seen running away to carry on crying at home, his board smashed to pieces and his dreams of becoming Welsh under sixteens champion this weekend dashed on the rocks with it.

A highly amusing incident. No further action is required, beyond severest piss-taking and immediate relegation to the bottom of the queue next time the Point breaks.

'They must like you,' he joked. 'Once the tide went out they collected the bits of your board. We're gonna nail it to the shop wall over there.' He pointed to a patch of wall above the surfboard rack.

I didn't like the sound of this.

'You can't do that,' I protested. 'My dad didn't know I was surfing.'

'We *can*. Tough shit. I'm sure he'll understand.'

As it happened, the old man did understand, and agreed to relay the story to my mother on my behalf. 'Then once she's calmed down I'll try and see if she'll still let you go to the Welsh tomorrow.'

This, of course, would have been the punishment to end all punishments – and not even my mother was cruel enough to risk that. She knew it would have consequences far outweighing the benefits – such as me running away, perhaps.

The main remaining problem was that my beloved board was no more – and I didn't have the money to buy another one. And even if I did, the time wouldn't exist to get used to it.

This was where Herbi came to the rescue.

'There's a piece-of-shit board out back, used to belong to Spud, which you can have for seventy quid,' he muttered.

'Spud? No way!' I almost jumped for joy. Spud was Matt Stephen, one of the best surfers in the country at the time – so to a kid my age the prospect of riding his old board in a surf contest was instantly enough to make me forget all the troubles of the day so far.

'Best of all,' Herbi continued, grinning at my dad and winking, 'I can arrange something for young Tom to do to get the money, once the exams are done.' That 'something', I learned months later – when the whole thing was but a memory and I'd fluked my way onto the Portugal trip with Spud's board – was whitewashing a roof for two pounds an hour. But that didn't matter. Again it was surely good for me in the grand scheme of things.

Promising never to take for granted how understanding people had been about this whole blunder, I accepted Herbi's terms and went home to pack for the Nationals trip, which hours before had seemed only possible in fantasy land. (This, by the way, was back when I used to get my – or rather my parents' – money's worth out of the event by actually making it past the first round.)

As I packed to leave for Pembrokeshire in the morning, my dad sat me down and requested that I made one promise. There were no negotiations on offer here. I had to agree to this or it was all off, and a weekend of revision would lie ahead.

'Sure. What is it?' I asked, tentatively.

'Promise me you'll never again try to get into the water at the Point by jumping off the rocks.'

Trying to hide my astonishment at how simple these terms were, I bit his hand off. Of course he had a deal.

And that is why this Point local will still never attempt the jump. To this day, I'll do it anywhere else on earth, but not at home.

Every time I'm running late to get in there I just remind myself of that fax, which stayed pinned to the notice board at Black Rock Surf Shop for years to follow – a reminder to look before you leap or, in my case, not to leap at all.

CHAPTER 11
THE GOLDIE LOOKIN' ISLAND

'Right then boys, which way now? Beauly, Dochgarroch and Drumnadrochit, or Dingwall and Strathpeffer? This road's going to the Muir of Ord...'

OK, I take it back. Cornish place names have nothing on these. A month after mine and Rich's 'Chasing Bill' adventure, bombing up the A9 towards Ullapool, I promised never to forget that this is always the point at which a trip to Scotland really gets underway: when you start having to decipher place names even us Welsh can't pronounce.

'Er... that way, I think...'

It can be a pretty gruelling journey, with the passing of Glasgow, Edinburgh and eventually Inverness lulling you into a false sense of security that you're nearing the surf. But it's not the case; the true cream of Scotland's waves are hours away from any of the cities – miles from the last outposts of mainstream life and off towards the upper extremes of weather, landscape and dialect. This land can both soothe you and drive you crazy at the same time – if the actual journey doesn't finish you off first.

This time though, my stoke was maintained by the fact that this was a journey I hadn't taken before. This time the call had come from Luke, and it wasn't to alert me to a Thurso swell. Our destination now was Ullapool and a ferry to the Isle of Lewis in the Outer Hebrides.

We had decided to try and learn from experience as far as that initial leg was concerned – taking the easy option of a flight up to Edinburgh, and hiring the most *bling* of people carriers: a gold eight-seater behemoth, labelled by Luke as the 'Goldie Lookin' Wagon' – until his mate and driver elect, a surfer from Sennen known as 'Triton', nearly killed us several times with his interpretation of night-time traffic dodging. From that moment on, Luke abandoned any loyalty to his music tastes and opted to label the KIA Sedona the 'Widow Maker' instead.

'Bloody hell, man! Can't you wait until after we've scored to kill us?' Luke yelled, as Glasgow Road finally fed us on to the M90 and a long, monotonous red-eyed drive towards our dawn sailing.

Along with Triton, Luke had brought along a professional surfer from Western Australia called Jason (who was staying in Devon to test-ride some of Luke's boards). Ever aware of walking the fine line between upping the numbers enough to make the rental cheaper and not wanting to turn us into 'rent-a-crowd', I'd given Math a last-minute call, rounding us off at five. Usually a team this size would make you the most unwelcome surf-trip crew on earth – but this was barely earth. We were heading to some of the least-populated surf locales yet discovered.

The finishing touches were put to the trip midway through the sickening sea-crossing to Stornoway, when another contact of Luke's rang to confirm he'd be showing us around – none other than the legendary Scottish surf explorer known as 'Dakker'. It seemed there wasn't a soul involved in British surfing that Luke didn't know. He'd pulled this trip together on word of an extraordinarily ferocious swell spinning down from the Arctic, and had put everything in place to score. One thing was clear – I had gotten myself on to a meticulously organised surf trip, on the tail of some of the heaviest waves in the country. The likelihood of this getting ugly was very high. And this time I had no excuse at all.

'So, spa, got a big-wave board then?' Luke jibed, nudging me as we sat on deck watching Math and Triton spew over a handrail and into the raging, green sea below.

'Yep. I've got a six-eight.'

'Safe! You're gonna be surfing hellman waves by the time the day's out.'

'That's what I was worried you'd say.'

'Worried? Good shit. Everyone's worried – that's fine. No one cares whether you're afraid. It's just whether you've got the guts to override the fear that matters.' He laughed and then turned to Jason. 'Duffy, you're afraid aren't you?'

Jason turned from looking pensively out to sea, his woolly hood moving an inch behind his neck so as to keep half of his tanned face hidden from view. 'Sorry mate. What's that?'

'Just telling Tom you're afraid of the surf out here. That it's normal, like.'

Jason smirked, his half-visible face not willing to reveal if he was joking or not. 'Speak for yourself, mate. I'm all over it.'

Luke laughed again. 'Fair enough. We're doomed with Duff on this trip. He'll be dragging us out to death bombs all week. Maybe Triton *should* have wrapped the Widow Maker into one of those lorries.'

Alarmingly, this trip had actually begun with a death.

In recent months I'd been earning a few quid by 'process serving'. Basically, via a mate of mine who'd got himself involved in freelance detective work, I'd been couriering legal papers to people. However, as you'd imagine, all the jargony law terms were horridly euphemistic in conveying the actual nature of this kind of work. A lot of the nastier court papers need to be 'served' on someone – namely the person who is 'subject' to whatever order had been issued by the grand, wig-wearing one. And a lot of people in their right mind don't like being served.

'Serving' involves confirming a person's identity, then informing them of the contents of the bundle of paper you're carrying, before leaving the documents in their presence. It's an adrenaline-filled job and the surf opportunities are immense. You'd go to county court, get the details of your next assignment, find the recipient, serve them and then, as most of my 'subjects' tended to be in the Vale of Glamorgan or West Wales, go surfing wherever you ended up. On occasions I'd turned serving missions into pleasant days out

– dropping dreadful news into people's laps before going for a meal somewhere with Breige. Someone would always need an injunction served in Cardiff on a Friday night and, as long as you found your man quickly (injunction recipients are almost always men), the rest of the evening was free to have a beer and some food or catch a film.

But one case, about a fortnight after the Severn Bore run, ended up a little more complicated. One evening I was called to urgently trace and serve a wealthy businessman who had tried to murder his wife on a weekend away. He'd bottled it at the last minute – and she'd woken up to find him standing over her, Macbeth-style, with a knife in his hands and a panicked look of indecision in his eyes. Understandably, while the Italian police (as the incident occurred in Milan) were deciding whether or not to send a fax to the local constabulary telling them to nick him, the wife decided an injunction might be an idea.

I'd been told by an ex-copper that if you accused someone of murder and they went nuts and tried to bop you, then it was usually an innocent person. The guilty tended to remain calm, but looked seedily anxious.

This man looked seedily anxious when I found him at home. There was no mistaking it whatsoever. He asked me where his wife was and I said I had no idea (she was at her brother's). He then thanked me and shook my hand. I could still feel the cold, clammy sweat of his palm as I was making the day's surfing plans the following morning – he'd obviously done exactly what she'd accused him of.

It was a sunny morning. The summer was hanging on, and a clean swell had given me and another supposed co-worker,

'Paparazzi Pete' (because he tried to freelance as a pap when he wasn't serving people), the idea of trying to score an off-limits beach break.

From Newport docks to Milford Haven's natural gas refinery, South Wales has always been proud of its heritage as an industrial coastline. The protected cliff walks of the Vale, Gower and south Pembroke are home to all sorts of secluded reef breaks fringed by gorgeous hills and muddy valleys, but once you've lived along the M4 corridor long enough, or have seen the factory plains by night, there's a beauty to be seen in some of these landscapes too. One of my favourite secret surf spots involved sneaking into one of these factory areas. This is another one I can't give you a location for, as the gang that surfs there regularly would slit my tyres and wax my windscreen. But I will say that the iron-ore pebbles and concrete platforms slowly being reclaimed by the sea, along with the backdrop of smoke and steam stacks, chimneys, floodlights, scaffolding and rising coal conveyor belts, always added a touch of the exotic to surfing so close to home. It was something different – and a deep-water pass behind the shoreline gave the waves some added power too. Rumour also had it that the impurities in the water kept it warm!

Getting access was always a hoot, and Pete was the best at it. As usual he took to the wheel up front, cramming me, Breige, the Bentley brothers (two local grommets from Porthcawl) and our boards in the back of his long-wheelbase van. Pete stuck a hard hat and high-vis tabard on and got ready to spout his best bullshit. At the entrance to the works, known as 'Checkpoint Charlie' to surfers, we were approached by a guard.

'Heads down, boys,' Pete whispered.

'All right mate, what's your business?'

'Morrisons Builders, come to fill in one of the cracked ramps. Sand's got under it again. Whoever does your foundations over there is a bloody idiot,' Pete bluffed.

'I see. Morrisons. Hang on a minute...' The guard walked slowly around the van before pacing back towards Pete's lowered window. 'Nothing flammable inside?'

The groms were trembling in their attempts to restrain themselves from laughing. I mimed slitting my throat to them and put my finger to my lips in a silent 'Shh'.

'And who are you then?' the guard carried on.

'Me?' Pete looked astonished.

'Yeah. You.'

'Well I'm Jim Morrison, int I!'

One of the Bentleys yelped and, for a moment, I was worried the guard had heard it. He hadn't, though. After a pause he waved us through, saying 'Sorry Mr Morrison – we have to ask. These surfin' types keep trying to get up to the beach behind the furnaces, see. You been on 'oliday lately, like?'

'I have as a matter of fact. Crete with the kids.' This was getting difficult even for me now.

'Aye – that explains it. Got a crackin' tan, you have, see. That's why I thought surfer for a second.'

'No. Sorry to disappoint.'

'No problem. Hope you can sort that concrete out. Ta da now.'

We were in.

'Jim Morrison' stuck the van out of sight behind a heap of rubble on the shoreline, which was essentially being used as a dumping ground for aggregate and slag. The light-hearted mood continued on to the sand as we readied to devour clean, late summer peaks with not another surfer in sight for miles in each direction. It was the first solid swell of September, and proof autumn would soon be blowing in some serious waves.

After two sessions, each a couple of hours long, broken by a sandwich in Pete's van, we were readying to leave, when I got the call.

'Mr Anderson? It's Sergeant Nicholas from South Wales Police here. Did you serve papers on a Mr — late last night? An injunction with power of arrest.'

'I did. Any problems?'

'You could say that.'

'Really? Is he OK?'

'Well, not really. He hanged himself about fifteen hours ago. Looks like you were the last person to see him alive. Do you, er, often have that effect on people?'

The day's surfing was forgotten immediately. Daily business to a senior copper maybe, but for me this was a heavy thing to be told so light-heartedly over the phone as I towelled sea water out of my hair.

The next day, when I walked in to the offices of the guy who'd been organising the work for me, it was to an apologetic look from his secretary.

'He says he's sorry,' she said, pursing her lips and arching her eyebrows matter-of-factly. 'Knows you like a trip away, though. Says take a few days off – he'll refund you if you want to go away somewhere – within reason, obviously.

Tough luck, that was. Shouldn't have given a case like that to someone just getting into the job.'

This seemed a reasonable suggestion, given that the last thing I felt like doing was trying to serve someone else that afternoon. And I'd seen the charts lately too – a huge swell was on its way. Yet again, opportunity was knocking.

The eerie sense of providence was compounded when I called Luke the same afternoon to suggest driving back down to South Devon for the swell.

'Bad idea, clart. I won't be here. But why not come to the Hebs with me?'

And that was that. The next episode had begun. Cornwall and Devon, the Severn Bore, Checkpoint Charlie – all part of a late summer push. But now it was time to embrace the cold again. My thoughts were turning back north, to a trip that had the potential to become the most intense I'd ever been on in the UK – if not ever.

We were now in high seas between Ullapool and Stornoway and the magnitude of the swell was really starting to show. A crashing reverberated through the ship as it dropped off the tip of a gargantuan breaker, only to wallop the next one head-on. A yell back in the galley preceded what sounded like the entire stock of plates and glasses falling to the floor and smashing to pieces.

The tone of excitement with which we'd laughed off Triton's driving had now been replaced with nervous expectation, and sombre dread.

'When we get to land we're all gonna have sea legs, probably too much to surf,' Luke warned.

This wasn't necessarily a bad thing, because the first part of the new swell had arrived in the form of near gale-force winds and sheets of sharp rain. As we drove off the ferry, the windscreen of the Widow Maker looked like some kind of fancy, permanent water feature, with a flow of rain run-off still overwhelming Triton's vision despite the wipers going at full speed.

When we arrived where we were going to stay – which was about 300 yards from the boat, although it took ten minutes to drive – Luke jumped out to knock on the door to 'Fair Haven', the place Dakker owned.

A few moments later he came back to the car to confirm that Dakker was waiting to show us in to a dorm room.

As I lugged my board bag through the corridor and upstairs, past walls of signed and snapped surfboards, a slim-built man with a boxer's nose and shoulder-length brown hair came up to me.

'Which one of ye poofs is from Porthcawl then?'

I looked at Dakker, not sure whether to 'fess up. 'Er, why?'

'D'you know someone called Rhino?' he asked, raising an eyebrow. I was sure this could only lead to something good – Rhino was loved by everyone he ever met on surf trips.

'Yeah, he's one of our best mates,' I replied, pointing to Math as well.

'Well, tell that wee bell-cheese to get his arse up here, tomorrow! He promised to come next time some Porthcawlies made it for a swell. Piker's probably scared. It's gonnae be huge in the next few days. I hope ye boys like yer surf life-and-death, like.'

Fortunately, he had decided that for the daylight hours remaining there was no point going surfing as the winds needed to blow over.

'Good in the morning, though,' he promised, before proposing to cook for us – an offer the seasick members of our party could only just conceal their reluctance to accept.

A big pot of curry was brought out. Dakker then fired up his VCR player and proceeded to spend the rest of the evening terrifying us with footage of monster swells, explaining how the one currently building on the horizon was 'as good as any of this here mush on me videos'.

The uneven coastlines in the more northern reaches of the world usually mean that somewhere will always have an offshore wind. Given the thumping south-westerly that had kicked up overnight, Dakker decided first of all to take us on a tour of some east-facing spots. This seemed a win–win situation for me, as it meant that besides the wind direction being way preferable to the fury that would now be annihilating the west coast, the swell would be considerably tamer too.

Following Dakker, who was in front in his own van, we drove out of the overcast and empty streets of Stornoway and on to a lane with tall hedges either side. Half a mile later, the hedges turned to dry-stone walls and then there was nothing around us but coarse grassland and the odd rocky outcrop. The van ahead then turned off at a crossroads, taking a right on to the intersecting road, which wasn't even paved. A red Royal Mail pillar box appeared a few hundred yards further on, squeezed into a break in the dry-stone wall, although there wasn't a building in sight.

The Widow Maker rocked from side to side as the road turned to cobblestones, dropping in and out of deep, puddle-filled potholes. Ahead of us the ocean, deep blue and covered by a thin film of mist, was getting nearer.

When we glimpsed the shoreline for the first time I realised there was to be no running from this swell. Even though we were on a coast facing almost the opposite direction to where the waves were coming from, lines were mounted as far as I could see. Dakker pulled up and got out of his van, gesturing to us to do the same. Triton opened the doors just in time for a pounding noise to echo across the road. It was from a wave, at least three times overhead, that had walloped a ledge out in front of us, its lip making direct contact with dry rock.

Half the rising mist was from the salty spray of waves exploding against the edge of a vast slab of flat granite, hundreds of yards wide.

'Good swell, boys!' Dakker declared with glee. 'Real power. Real raw. Saddle back up. I know where to meet this baby!'

Another wave rumbled its way across in front of us, blowing scented sea air and spray upwards into the low clouds of fizzling vapour. I could feel it breaking through the ground beneath my feet. Dakker was already back in his van and driving.

There were, apparently, dozens of world-class reefs and point breaks along these eastern shores, but we only got as far as the first one.

'No way!' Triton called out from the front, as Dakker bleated his horn ahead of us. 'Sick!'

'Aaah! We're in there.' Jason, otherwise contemplatively quiet, exclaimed.

Across a cobbled beach in front of us a peak rose out of the dark ocean surface and pitched forward. The lip feathered for a moment in the wind and then chucked, leaving a tube wide enough for anyone to stand tall in. The wave then turned in on itself and rolled, still wide open, towards a deep water channel, before chucking the air and water it had stored within out into the open air. After that it clamped shut, disappearing into nothing but a patch of turbulent foam over the reef in front of it.

My jaw dropped in awe. Although it was enormous, the wave had broken so cleanly, so wide and with such compliant symmetry that any surfer able to get to their feet would surely be able to get barrelled to the brink of their sanity.

'Well,' Dakker chuckled, walking over to us. 'Will that do? What are ye waiting for, boys! It's even good enough for me to join you.'

Each time the ledging right-hander spat, we lost a little more of the patience needed to wriggle into heavy, five-mil winter suits.

Jason was mumbling sweet nothings to himself: 'Perfect pits on the first day... *Siiick*.'

Despite having the least experience of neoprene, he was first into the water and screamed with cold shock as he jumped the shore break, but soon forgot the pain in his toes as another one turned inside-out only yards in front of him. Given that Jason rode this kind of stuff for a living, it was clear we were about to see a real show.

It was just as well he did go out first, because he did the rest of us the favour of discovering the nasty rip that was trying to pull you behind the peak. The reason for this was the immediate increase in depth as soon as you jumped over the shore break. The wave was rising out of open ocean, straight on to a clearly defined outcrop of rock just beneath the surface. This was the reason it was able to harness such energy onto a concentrated spot. But all the disturbed water around would take you in a range of unpredictable directions.

We all had to take our share of beatings before anyone wired the place enough to start really charging it. Again, the man for the job was Jason. Just as it was starting to look as if this place would be too much of a challenge to get the hang of during our first session, he stumbled on the key. Almost caught in the way of a solid set, he was stuck paddling up the face of double-overhead waves with a real risk of getting pulled over with the lip. Jason had other ideas though, and instead of diving through the face to the safety of the other side he about-turned and took off – not so much jumping to his feet as dropping them down onto the board. Somehow his rail connected and he swooped under a twisting lip, gaining pace like a runaway train as the tube pulled him towards the shoulder.

The rest of us were ecstatic just at the sight of that one and we began screaming like playground children.

'Up the Duff, mate,' Luke punned as Jason sunk next to him.

'I think you just named the spot for me, boys,' Dakker grinned.

Jason had cracked it. The only way to stay out of the rip and get into the best waves was to place yourself perilously close to the impact zone and to hook into the wave at the last possible moment before it broke. It was easy enough for him, but the balance required to negotiate a drop like that with so much water moving around you is something that takes years to acquire, and something that comes a little quicker when you grow up in West Oz. For the rest of us the session was going to be utterly hair-raising.

All this terror wasn't without its rewards. The adrenaline that came with successfully making it to the bottom of one of these heaving waves reached the bottom of the soul, and left you hopelessly hooked on trying to get another one.

The machine-like predictability of where and how the wave would break also played into the hands of those less familiar with such conditions. Once you'd gone for a few the place began to feel more inviting, and we each took turns trying to slow ourselves for the tube. Within the hour I had started daring to hold myself back enough to see the lip throwing in front of me, and to hear the rest of the world's background noise getting cut off by soundproof tunnels of water.

As we toyed with how deep we could adjust our own personal lines, Jason set about pushing the boundaries of what you could do with this wave full stop. Anchoring his arm in the face, right up to the shoulder, he'd stall himself until the foam vortex in the furthest recesses of the barrel began causing his fins to shudder. Then he'd start extending and recoiling himself, driving desperately for the exit – often with such bravado that he'd only escape with inches to spare as the final section slammed shut.

And so it was that our love affair with the 'Up the Duff' right-hander began. It turned out we'd only had a taster of it that evening, as the wind dropped over the coming days to make the place even more perfect, and easier to ride.

The rest of us remained in awe of Jason's knack for making things look simpler than they really were. By the mid-point in the session he was getting tubed on just about any wave he picked. His control of where he was, and how he was moving, was total.

'Up the Duff' was an ideal wave if you liked the stomach-churning experience of dropping straight into the barrel, but for me the next two days of surfing were as adrenaline-filled as any period I'd experienced before – anywhere. The wave would swing wide on approach, making for a real heart-in-the-mouth take-off as you angled headlong towards a warping section.

But, then again, I had it easy. Math and Luke were goofyfoots and had to surf with their backs to the wave, meaning they had to go through the whole process without being able to really square their bodies up properly. They needed intuition in abundance to survive the sessions – as well as a gung-ho attitude.

Jason's antics had attracted some of the hard core local surfing population, here to see their waves being torn apart by this world-class surfer. Two guys in a converted camper van had arrived on the beach and suited up. One was a photographer, called Mark, who swam into the line-up to score in-the-tube photographic evidence of the Australian's prowess, while his mate Jim calmly took to the line-up on a big yellow pintail.

Softly spoken and patient, Jim commented on the quality of the waves, exchanged conversational pleasantries with

Dakker and then paddled for one. It was a middle-of-the-range set, which had sucked itself deep behind the reef. Fully expecting Jim to get crucified, I started wincing as I saw the wave fold. With an instinctive understanding of the spot though, Jim had gotten himself into it early and gently rose to his feet. As his board caught the trough of the wave he held his weight over his back foot and waited confidently, knowing what was to happen next. He'd read it perfectly: the barrel poured around him, breaking several feet beyond the nose of his board, as he transferred his weight back to the front and shot out into the deep-water channel with barely a change of facial expression. As if that wasn't impressive enough, the last touch to Jim's tube riding had been the epitome of grace under pressure – he'd clasped his hands neatly behind his back before coming out, no doubt giving his mate Mark a better surf shot than anything Jason had done all trip.

As the rest of us stared in amazement, Dakker let out a rallying cry:

'Yeeeah! Pro surfer rippin' the place to pieces, but you can always trust the island boys to get the wave of the day!' Obviously spurred on himself, he then turned to paddle for the next wave, which had suffered from the foam Jim's had left behind. This time the lip threw out, uncontrolled and malevolent, ensuring there was no chance of making the drop.

But that didn't stop Dakker. Once he realised he was doomed, he just made a star shape with his arms and legs and threw himself into the air, almost completing a full somersault on his way to the reef below.

He popped up spluttering, shook the water out of his hair and then yelled, 'Your turn, boys! Time to get kamikaze! Who's 'avin' it next?'

The relief I felt when the swell dropped was manifest. For three days we'd gone to sleep shivering and shattered from hours of oceanic pummelling, only to wake up to the sight of Dakker standing in the middle of the dorms making such declarations as, 'Still ten foot of swell making it round the butt. Wind's good. We're missing waves already boys, let's get 'avin' it!'

That last bit – ''avin' it' – had become his catchphrase and a phrase I was coming to dread as it meant being expected to throw life and limb to the mercy of more pounding reef-break waves.

But on day five things had finally changed as Dakker proposed taking us over to the other side of the island for a whole new set of spots. (The range of surfing possibilities in Scotland's more remote islands can be an unsettling thought, if you entertain it too long. It makes you feel like dropping everything to move up north and start exploring.)

The wind had dropped and, as we stocked up on bananas, chocolate bars and soft drinks at the petrol station on the edge of Stornoway, I could feel both the sea and land around us welcoming in high pressure.

Before bombing off ahead of us again, Dakker explained his habit of driving really fast whenever he took people surfing: 'It's so that no bell-cheeses from the mainland can remember how to get there again.' Given that this morning we would be following him through the middle of the Isle of Lewis and a winding road of hills with hardly any cars, I was a little uneasy with the proposition – especially considering Triton's propensity to endanger life by driving through red lights.

'Do many surfers know their way around here?' Luke asked Dakker.

'No. These islands are some of the least-known coastlines in Europe,' our host explained. 'And I really want it to stay that way. I love how you still have to search for the spots up here, without yer *Stormriders* and yer guidebooks. Up here we just 'ave it good and proper.'

A chorus of ''Avin' it!' came from Math and Luke in the back of the Widow Maker.

Dakker continued: 'There's still that element of discovery up here. And you tell me of a place that still makes ya feel that? Not even Caithness and Thurso these days. And I get stoked seeing people finding waves instead of looking them up. Real surfing, my boys.'

As we chased him around the first bend of many, and the g-force gripped me, I wondered what prompted people like Dakker to surf such freezing conditions, often all alone. Was any wave worth that lifestyle? But the answer was obvious. This guy got to ride raw, open-ocean juice probably almost as often as you could in Indonesia or Jason's home of Western Australia – and without the crowds. He was just lucky not to really mind the cold and seemed to have the required screw loose to thrive on having these landscapes as home.

The road ahead threaded its way beneath us, as slopes of thin, short grass and scrub rolled away to each horizon. Sometimes little walls appeared at the sides, as well as bigger hills and outcrops, with unsecured scree-slopes that often spilled onto the carriageway. At the highest points the greenery would disappear, leaving just plains of grey rock and rubble. Signs of life were minimal.

'This is like the surface of the moon, man,' whispered Jason, leaning his forehead against the side window. 'There's nothing like it in Oz.'

I remembered an anecdote Rhino had told me about when he made the journey from east coast to west coast on the Isle of Lewis. He'd gone via the north coast of the island, past an outer head known as the 'Butt of Lewis'. Simply a geographical term in the local dialect, his party had found great humour in this signpost – especially as they had another Porthcawl surfer named Gary Lewis in their midst. Rhino got the idea of making Gary pull a moony next to the sign 'Butt of Lewis' and for the others to take a picture. Gary agreed. It was with embarrassment that the group of guffawing surfers, cameras in hand, spotted a local dog-walker passing by. The dog walker seemed unsurprised. 'Another Lewis, eh boys?' the gentleman had apparently noted. 'Aye, we get them all the time.'

There would be no such opportunities for us though, even if we had had a Lewis with us, as we were being given a crash course in the more direct route from east to west – almost literally a few times, as Triton swerved around unfamiliar bends and kinks, desperately trying to keep the rear of Dakker's van in view.

'This guy's driving is deadly,' our pilot complained above the sound of screeching rubber.

'That doesn't mean yours has to be,' Luke barked.

'It does if we wanna find out where he's going.'

As the west coast drew near, the island was being blessed with more and more greenery. I wondered if it was because the moisture-laden sea air got pushed in so often by the prevailing Atlantic winds. A couple of trees started appearing here and there, and then we arrived at a road that was running south to north – pretty much along the furthest shoreline of the Isle of Lewis.

Without indicating and using only the barest tap of his breaks, Dakker swung onto this road heading north. The road was so long, and flat, that we were able to keep tabs on him from a good way back, and Triton took the liberty of negotiating the T-junction with a bit more care.

Then, after a few undulations in the road, Dakker, again without any warning, veered sharply to the left and promptly bumped up and over a mini sand dune. It took us twenty seconds to reach the same point, by which time he was gone. Triton tentatively mounted the same dune, just in time for us to glimpse Dakker going over another one.

Once we'd repeated the process a few times and it was clear we weren't going to keep up with him any more, a sudden change of heart seemed to occur. He stopped up ahead and proceeded to wait for us, sitting against the bonnet of his van and enjoying the mid-morning rays.

'I'm gonna show you a 'no swell' spot called Nuggets today,' he explained once we arrived within earshot, before climbing back in to his van and setting off again.

This unexpected bit of off-roading brought us right up to the coastline and the breathtaking realisation that we were the only evidence of civilisation for miles. No roads, no buildings, no jet trails in the clear sky – no ships on the sunlit horizon. A piece of headland eventually halted our progress, leaving us overlooking a bay of light-blue water with no apparent surf. I'd decided Dakker was mad long ago, but decided to trust his decision to wait for low tide and the appearance of a 'fast, spitting sandbar that'll break yer boards'.

While we waited, trying to enjoy the rarity of what was now a warm day in one of the northernmost isles in the UK, an inquisitive generation of rabbits began hopping towards us. Dakker started making noises about killing a few for our evening meal but managed to read the looks on our faces well enough to realise it wasn't our idea of a fun pastime while waiting for the waves.

A few sets had started to feather off the rock face to our north, so Luke and Jason decided to paddle out.

Within the hour the rest of us, including Dakker, had raced to join them. The sandbar appeared within one quick surge of tide, to reveal a set-up of head-high, barrelling right-handers.

'This is the Scottish Superbank,' Dakker quipped. I could see the irony in this comparison – the real Superbank, in Queensland, Australia, was a scrappy, sub-tropical, 200-surfer free-for-all. We had the place to ourselves.

The water may have been fifteen degrees colder than the namesake but, as far as the wave went, Dakker's comparison wasn't that far off. As the turquoise sets spun down the line, they kept scouring up little patches of gold sand from the bottom. Although still tubing like mad in places, this was a much more high-performance wave than Up the Duff, and everyone was stoked with the opportunity to loosen up. Triton and Jason were smacking every section they could find, smoothly cracking their boards through the thin, clear-water lip, showering the rest of us with sunlit spray.

Meanwhile, Math and Luke set themselves further down the line, pulling into the racy end-section on their backhand – enjoying the benefits of the soft sandy bottom and gentle wipeouts.

Dakker and his mates had dubbed this place 'Nuggets' partly because of the golden, medallion-like swirls in the wave faces, but also because fools gold could be found on the beach a couple of times a year.

'The right swells bring these little shingles of rocks in,' he explained, 'and some of them look like gold.'

'I like the sound of that,' replied Luke. 'Can we call this spot something else as well though? How does the "Goldie Lookin' Sandbar" sound to you?'

'Dunno, man. Ye boys already named "Up the Duff" for me. I'll think about it.'

Nuggets, the Goldie Lookin' Sandbar, whatever it ended up being known as, worked for hours that afternoon – right through low tide and halfway towards mid – leaving us all approaching the point of being completely surfed out. Best of all, the only witnesses to it all were the rabbits and a family of goats that had grazed their way over to inspect this unusual interruption to their daily routine.

We only had one day left on the island after this, although the general consensus was that we could have gladly gone home then and there. Cold water and hours of steaming surf had taken a heavy toll on our bodies.

'I hope the swell goes tomorrow,' Triton groaned, as we packed our stuff away for the drive back to Stornoway and our bunk beds, which in our state of fatigue seemed impossibly far off in the future.

'Better get on your knees and pray then, soft cocks,' laughed Dakker. 'It's already flat everywhere else, so it can only pick up again.'

That night he showed us more footage of the winter swells. Ten foot, twelve foot, bigger – and each time the locals were still on it. We even saw footage of a deadly suckout breaking at fifteen-foot plus. Behind the trembling camcorder you could hear Dakker crying out to himself in awe, as he watched waves that would test the resolve of even the world's greatest surfers. You could hardly blame him for not wanting to attempt such high-stakes conditions alone – even though he claimed to have been tempted a few times.

'Pros have been out there for a look,' Dakker said, 'but none of them have taken off. Not yet, anyway. When they reached the line-up all they did was turn back.'

The swell did drop the following day after all – giving us a chance to take a walk around Stornoway before packing up the Widow Maker for the return journey. Dakker's pledge that it could only get bigger again may well have been right, but that wasn't going to happen in time to worry us.

Yesterday's generous weather had retreated, meaning it was business as usual with grey skies and the occasional shower blown in from the sea. The town centre was positively bustling for somewhere so remote, with a host of souvenir shops if you felt like buying something silly and Hebridean to take home. Pubs were preparing for a day's trade, as well as the cafes, while the bleating of seagulls reminded us that a harbour was just the other side of the main strip.

For the main post of civilisation on Lewis, it was still a tiny town – you could map it in your mind after one quick walk. An hour later it was reducing even more in size from the balcony of the return ferry, before finally dropping from view, soon to be replaced by Ullapool and the mainland. I felt a pang of parting sorrow. Something of your soul gets inextricably linked to the Outer Scottish Isles, taking a hold on you, and I knew I'd long for Stornoway again soon.

As the thick, glacial hills and cacophonous place names finally gave way to the banks of Loch Ness on our journey back to Edinburgh, I began to reflect on what had been waiting for me in the Outer Hebrides – genuine world-class surf, without even breaking out our passports. The chance to see and surf bits of coastline so secluded that human tracks were nowhere to be seen. And the thrill of the road and that sense of quest that had become an essential part of my take on the surfing lifestyle. All of this, yet again, had been available in the UK. The idea of that being possible had seemed pretty alien to me in the spring – but now, I realised, I was well on my way to re-shaping the way I saw home and its opportunities.

With the relentless fuss of Edinburgh life around us once again, Triton searched for the rental car drop-off spot, while Jason phoned home to tell his folks about the trip – only to learn that a twelve-foot swell had just hit West Oz.

'Do you care?' I asked him.

'About what?'

'Missing it – the swell.'

He didn't even think before responding. 'Not even! This place is sick. I'm coming back next year…'

So, I thought, am I.

CHAPTER 12
IRELAND: WAITING FOR
WHOKNOWSWHAT...

'I can see why they call this the bloody *Emerald Isle*. Greenest place on earth – it's just that people overlook the *reason* for all that green. This place rains more than anywhere I've ever been. It's official!'

I was rambling, nearing the point at which I could take no more. Five days in Ireland – and I'd spent most of my time in a stuffy car staring at the wipers as they pushed away a constant layer of rain. Of course, this would all have been worthwhile if it had been for the sake of pumping surf, but so far I'd seen nothing but a load of onshore mush and none of it rideable. So far the catchphrase of the trip had become Mrs Doyle's legendary offer of *'Tea, fathers?'* – just about summing up the sense of cabin fever that comes with being penned in by such relentless torrents.

The Outer Hebrides could have been like this for me, I know, but they weren't, and would forever be seen as

221

idyllic in my mind. But Ireland, so far, had some catching-up to do.

Behind the wheel was Rhydian, a friend from back home, who had recently begun developing some Irish connections. He was here visiting the family of his girlfriend, Fiona, who was from County Claire. He'd done well for himself – County Claire was home to some of the best surf in Europe. However, today it was nowhere in sight.

This afternoon, after driving up and down the coast around Lahinch, one of Ireland's premier surf towns, we'd grown fed up with increasingly futile attempts to find somewhere to surf, and had jumped on a boat to the Arran Islands. Rhyd claimed it was because the place was one of Ireland's most remote pieces of land, and that the beauty of the islands would rival even those of outer Scotland. I knew, though, that the real reason to go there was that Inis Oírr was the setting of the fictional 'Craggy Island' from *Father Ted*.

'Tea, fathers?'

Now on our way back by boat after walking along rows of dry-stone walls, none of which served as any refuge from the buffeting sea breezes, I was watching the wreck of the *Plassey* go past us to the right. This was the rusted, skeletal ship visible from the sky at the start of the TV show's opening credits and I was staring at its corroding hull in hope. To Rhyd it was just another of the important sights for a *Father Ted* fan, but for me it was a reminder that these seas, at the moment obstinately devoid of any swell above a light bit of wind-chop, could produce *serious* waves from time to time. It had been wrecked nearly fifty years ago, but since that time the surf had given it such a hammering that the *Plassey* now sat well above the high-tide mark. So far our own boat-ride had been much more straightforward.

Even today, with nothing registering on the swell charts, you could feel that this ocean was capable of coming to life with little warning. We bore east, towards the small harbour at Doolin in which Rhyd had left the car. There was no sign of land in either direction until another rolling wall of mist broke to reveal a series of dark shapes, looming on the horizon.

'That's the Cliffs of Moher, man,' Rhyd whispered through a single, drawn-out breath, as if the landmark might hear us from over a mile away. 'Biggest waves ever ridden in Europe, probably – right there, in front of the spike.'

He pointed through the grey, salt-scented afternoon, at a stack of rock that sat just off one of the 400-foot cliff faces. Thin pillars of mist and sea vapour hung between them, steadily rising up, suspended against the wind.

In recent years a bunch of local surfers, along with a few international visitors, had begun pioneering a wave that broke just off the foot of these cliffs. Known as 'Aileen's', it was a peak that only began to show once the swell was already way beyond anything most people would dare ride. Photos had begun to shake the surfing world of riders at the bottom of waves that looked akin to anything that had yet been discovered in the Pacific Ocean – which until recently was believed to be the world's hub for big-wave surfing.

The kamikaze act practiced at places like Aileen's was nowhere near what surfers like me did on a daily basis. Aileen's at its most furious would pull waves through its line-up at such speeds that it was almost impossible to catch them – which was why the surfers there would often use jet skis to whip each other in to the peak early. This meant you could get ahead of the avalanche of water that chased any surfer brave (or stupid) enough to catch a wave here. That avalanche of water was not something to naïvely joust with either; it was easy to get slammed straight into the mighty Cliffs of Moher, which in the dead of winter, with thirty feet of swell running, could easily mean you'd ridden your last ever wave.

One of the first surfers of Aileen's was none other than Al Mennie, one of my co-victims at that ridiculous West Wales surf comp. In the years since he had left contest surfing behind and focused his act on chasing some of the nastiest surf spots on the planet – having even made the shortlist for the prestigious Billabong-sponsored XXL Global Big Wave Awards. He'd become one of the first European surfers to really make it on the world scene, showing up at some of the most famous big-wave destinations on the planet, such as Waimea Bay in Hawaii, the northern Californian horror show known as Mavericks and the open-ocean peaks of Mexico's Todos Santos.

Rather him than me, I thought, as our boat swung towards the north to Doolin and yet more dormant surf spots.

Again there was little to suggest to the untrained eye that even this small alcove, protected by an uninhabited island in which the boat was docking, could be home to two more of Ireland's most beautiful waves. One was on the island itself: a ledging peak, known to be sinister and board-breaking, dubbed 'Crab Island'. Then just to the south of that slab of rock, and visible from the quay, was a right-hand point.

Today both were home only to a few inches of swell, but the latter was often mistaken for Thurso in photographs. Both awed and frustrated by the potential of what was around, I trudged towards the car. It was all well and good to get up close and personal with the ocean (and a boat-ride like the one we'd just taken always ensures that), but to me it would be worthless if I didn't get to ride a few waves soon.

Rhyd wasn't feeling the same pressure as me. He came here all the time and had surfed just about everywhere in County Claire, as well as across the Dingle Peninsula to the south. But my stay was limited to just this week – by a famous, tight-fisted Irishman, as it happened. I was here after spotting a one-pound Ryanair flight from Bristol to Shannon, the 'home airport' of Michael O'Leary's infamous airline. Rhyd had picked me up, having driven his own car over, and had already delayed his ferry back to try and score a few waves with me. And since my £2.60 return flight was in three days' time, we needed to get busy.

Winding our way in Rhyd's car through more saturated greenery, back towards Ennis and the heart of County Claire, Rhyd still had other ideas.

'If we head off towards Corofin, we can go look at Father Ted's actual house!' he explained, animatedly. 'That part of the set is on the mainland, miles from the sea. It's in Kilnaboy. Good name for a village, eh! Once in a lifetime opportunity this, mate.'

I stared out the window yet again at Lahinch, a beach town in total hibernation – surf schools, shops and hostels were all closed while the wind blew sand, mist, rain and foam in off the brown ocean. There wasn't much else on offer, and if there was one perk to this mini-obsession we were developing for the classic Channel 4 comedy, it was that it did kind of make the most of the dreary conditions.

'This is why they chose County Claire to film the show,' Rhyd explained. 'It's the wettest, greyest, greenest part of Ireland!'

'I already told you that a few hours ago,' I muttered.

When dawn broke the following day, that same wet weather had led to yet another of Rhyd's once-in-a-lifetime opportunities. We ought, he explained, to offer to carry out a quick 'favour' for our hosts before going in search of surf for the day.

Fiona's dad, Pat, needed a hand moving something. Forty cows.

'It'd be a real help to him if you could lend a hand,' Fiona explained, as we finished a coffee in the kitchen of her parents' farmhouse in the tiny village of Moyhill. The River Shannon, just behind Moyhill, was getting a bit feisty and Pat's cows needed herding before there was a chance of flooding.

I was offered a rod, with which to hit the animals apparently, and a pair of wellies. That was all you needed, it seemed, to be plunged headlong into the world of free-range farming in these parts. Ten minutes later we were running across a crater-filled field with confused cattle spreading in every direction.

Pat had tried to explain to us the principle of cow-herding, with the help of a sheepdog who seemed to know even more about it than him. But it wasn't much use. A big part of my inability lay in my unwillingness to hit any of the cows – even though Pat kept reassuring me that they couldn't feel much. He was probably right but that didn't make whacking a living creature any easier.

Two hours later, we'd moved just twelve of them.

You may think that at this point I'd have felt frustrated – yet again surfing seemed a very far-off prospect. But it didn't bother me at all. The break was welcome. As much as is possible when chasing cows around a field on the banks of the River Shannon, I was having some sort of epiphany. Surfing was speaking to me again.

What other reasons, I wondered, could someone possibly have for getting into this situation? Nothing else in my life had my attention to such an extent that it could lead me out to run cattle in the rain-saturated, agricultural fields of western Ireland. Who needed the backpacker trails of Asia or Latin America, or the open roads of the USA and Australia? This was travel – of a more wild and far-flung nature than a lot of transcontinental trips could offer anyway.

When we got back to the house after walking through the village of Bunratty to grab lunch – that was where we'd left the last five cows – Rhyd checked the swell charts again. There was still nothing, although finally a slight change was on the cards for tomorrow:

'Wave period shoots right up over night,' he pointed out, tapping the screen of Pat's monitor, while Fiona and the rest of the family looked on with no idea what he was saying. 'So that could be the day. Still gonna be windy, but look how craggy this coastline is.'

'Craggy Island!' I interrupted, and Fiona's mum, Sue, chuckled. The whole family knew Rhyd and I couldn't get *Father Ted* out of our minds.

Rhyd gestured to the outline of County Claire on the left of the screen: 'That's what makes it so good for waves. We'll find somewhere with a good wind direction whatever happens. It's gonna rain again, but who cares?'

'OK. Sounds good to me. Let's forget surfing for the day and hit it with a vengeance tomorrow.'

'That's the spirit,' he congratulated me.

'Good way of doin' things,' Pat added. 'Maybe sometimes you push a bit hard, you know, then it's not gonna work for you. Give it a bit of patience. Trust the waves, like, then who knows what could happen?'

Wise words for someone who has never surfed – so much so that it made me wonder for a moment if he was talking about the cows again.

Pat wanted to thank us for helping him herd the cattle that morning, so at teatime he offered to take us to 'see the dogs' in Limerick.

'My friend's got a dog in the seventh race,' he explained. 'Lucky number. He's hopin' it'll place something tonight. Are you a lucky man, Tom?'

'Not so far,' I frowned. 'But that's always liable to change, eh?'

'Of course. Remember what I said earlier. Maybe this is the change of fortunes you need.'

We hopped into his Land Rover, and after adjusting the cushion on his seat and rubbing his back, Pat fired the engine up and we were off. Limerick was a short run in the opposite direction to Bunratty, which took us past Cratloe and then through a series of busier roads until we were going right through the city centre. We crossed a well-lit bridge, which took us over the River Shannon – now a little wider but more under control than she had been when marauding through Pat's land back in Moyhill and annoying the cows. As in Wales, every road sign was repeated in Gaelic, and before long one in bolder lettering announced our arrival in one of Ireland's biggest cities:

Limerick – *Luimneach*

Limerick Greyhound Stadium was hardly noticeable. If Pat hadn't known where to go, we'd never have found it ourselves. He pulled in to a small, warehouse-like building with no obvious name. A man with old clothes and a weathered face surrounded by wild and wiry black hair walked up to us.

'Hello Pat,' he said. 'What race'll you be stayin' till? I need to know where to park you.'

'Oh, the seventh,' Pat replied.

'Oh yes, John's dog's runnin', eh? Right, pull in over there.' The man pointed to a space and we pulled up. At the end of the building was an outdoor yard and then a turnstile that released us onto a walkway that went right the way around the track, which seemed to have been inconspicuously smuggled in to the middle of a block of other city buildings, like a dirty secret. At the other side of the track to us was a stand and a few booths, most of them home to bookmakers.

Fiona and Rhyd went to get cups of tea, while Pat explained to me the difference between betting the 'Tote' and going to a private bookie. The sole traders looked intimidating, each of them lined up in a row along the bottom of the stand shouting odds with the manner of auctioneers. The 'Tote', meanwhile, was the safer, computer-run system, which involved walking up to an indoors counter where a bored girl was writing text messages and chewing a piece of gum as if it was the only thing worthy of her full attention.

'Are you good at bettin'?' Pat asked. 'Have you got a system?' Fiona had told me that he liked taking new people to the dogs because he thought they often had fresher instincts than hardened gamblers. She'd warned me he'd probably watch my every move to see if he could 'learn something'.

'I'll probably read up on the dogs and try and work out their times and history,' I offered, meekly. 'Is there a programme?'

Pat stared bemusedly at me. 'Oh. That method, eh? Better watch the dogs come out then, too. See how many times they wee, if they look excited, focused.' Then he walked outside.

Fiona came over with some teas, holding a ticket stub in her mouth. She'd bet already. No system, just the first dog name to appeal to her. *Tonetta Breeze*. 'You can't work out anything,' she explained, shaking her head. 'Otherwise we'd be here every night making a fortune. All the bettin' does is help you enjoy the race.'

All the same, I decided to take it as seriously as I could. I watched the first race, which made me gasp at how fast the creatures could run, and then settled on an idea. Number five had seemed destined to win the race from the off simply because of the angle she (I checked the dog's gender in the programme) had been able to take in to the first bend.

Without saying any more I made for the Tote. Rhyd passed me, cursing having lost three euros. He suggested a side bet on which one of us had done the best by the end of the night which, given his handicap after having lost a few euros already, seemed a fair offer.

'You're on,' I nodded and turned to the clerk to make my first call: 'Number five; three euros.'

'Each way?' she queried, without even looking up.

'Er... yeah?'

'Six euros please.'

'What? How'd that work?'

'Each way – three to win, three to place.'

I remembered my one and only flutter on the Grand National back home – the same thing had happened to me then. Thinking it a blessing I knew so little about gambling, I reached for my cash, then walked back to the edge of the track.

It was about five minutes to the next race, which I spent outside talking to Rhyd about our surf prospects for tomorrow. If we didn't strike lucky, there'd be one day left before Ryanair packed me into one of their metal boxes and posted me back to Bristol.

'We shouldn't stress about it,' he reminded me. 'Once the swell arrives there'll be somewhere to surf whatever the wind. Trust me. This place absolutely pumps. I've driven past so many possible surf breaks. It'll be insane.'

'Have you bet this time?' I asked, wanting to change the subject for fear of getting up false hopes yet again.

'No,' he replied, firmly. 'I'm taking one off. Gonna wait for the luck to return. I've been here enough times to know how this shit works. It'll be the same with the surf. Don't worry though, I'll have you. I know how competitive you are. That's why you get so tense about surfing.'

'Shut up, I'm not competitive.'

'Whatever.'

I'm not sure why I was trying to argue this one – if I wasn't competitive then why did I get so forlorn losing? But then I had just spent half a year trying to reassess my competitive streak, perhaps hoping it might drop off like an unwanted tail.

But then my dog won and I felt that surge of adrenaline.

'Now we'll see if you're lucky,' said Pat as I grinned my way past him to go and place another bet. 'Try and do it twice. I'd stick with number five now. It likes you.'

If I couldn't win at surfing, then maybe I should take up something else.

Staring at the list of dogs for the next race, something in the back of my mind was distracting me. Rhyd's jibe was echoing through my head. He had a point. My lowest moments in surfing had always involved contests – while travel, it seemed, especially foreign travel, had been behind all of my best memories. This year I was addressing that dependence on foreign travel at least, but was I really any way towards shaking off my contest demons?

Without betting again, I wandered back out of the cafe-cum-bookmakers into the crisp night-time air. The dogs for the next race were being walked across to the starting cages by their owners. Pacing along the edge of the track, I watched the steam from my breath and sunk my hands deeper into my pockets for warmth. A smile caught the corner of my mouth as I thought this over.

In a way, I thought, I'd actually loved *hating* going to contests in Britain. Ever since the year I first caught the travel bug, when a month in France and Portugal had ended with a trip straight to Newquay.

Now it seemed funny. When I was sixteen I'd qualified for two junior surf contests, one near Lisbon and the other in the French town of Lacanau. I'd packed my bags and put together an itinerary that would keep me away from home for the entire school holidays, ending with the British Nationals in Newquay – round one of which took place on the Thursday I was due to get me GCSE results. (This should have meant a lot to me, as I'd learn whether my dad's incentive scheme had worked).

However, giddy with the joys of living out of a suitcase for weeks, of being away from my family and surfing every hour I could find – as well as discovering the thrill of wanderlust – I hadn't given the British Nationals, competing or my exams a moment's thought. Until at ten in the morning, when in knee-high surf and with rain falling so hard you couldn't see more than twenty yards, I drew Rich Grove in the first heat of the event.

I lost to him and a young blonde kid from Newquay who I'd never seen before, and suddenly had four more days in Surf City UK to think about it. Quick as any poison, homesickness welled within me from deep down, paralysing time.

From a payphone on Headland Road, I learned that a train ticket back early would cost £137. One hundred and thirty-seven pounds to get from Cornwall to Wales! It was preposterous.

But I almost considered trying to find the money for it when I made my second phone call. I dialled home to learn of my exam results. I'd got the grades my parents had hoped for, as had most of my school friends. My mother had seen a good crew of them, including Rhyd, and they'd asked after me. Apparently they were all throwing a beach party: a summer blast to live long in their teenage memories.

And I was stuck in Newquay after a month on the road, reeling. This exorbitant fee, this ransom, would only be good enough for a thirteen-hour journey with six changes anyway. I was completely defeated and didn't even have the emotional energy required to cry.

At least my dad had managed to come up with a wonderfully inappropriate consoling message.

'Hey, there's one piece of good news,' he reminded me (besides the exam results, which I'd already forgotten).

'What?'

'Remember I said you could keep that surfboard if you got the right grades?'

'Yeah. The one I broke into four pieces,' I mumbled back down the heavy plastic handset.

'Yeah, that one,' he replied, coolly. 'Well, look on the bright side. At least you don't have to pay me for it now!'

I can't remember if I hung up. The horror of being stuck miles away from home – my first taste of the flip-side to travel, and millionth taste of the flip-side to competing – is by far the dominant memory.

But I'd absolved myself of this loathing of Cornwall now. The depression of that afternoon had been part of the experience. If you wanted to live your life from getaway to getaway you had to *love it all*. Love the losing, the things that didn't work out, love the loneliness.

I jumped as the bell sounded to signal that the next race was due to start. With a whoosh the hare was released, the echo of it tore around the track and conducted itself, like an approaching train, through the rail in front of me. Inside the cages the greyhounds started whimpering with excitement, scratching at doors they knew would open any second.

Love the rain, I thought. Love the cold. Love each and every mishap that will occur as a surfer in these hostile waters. It's all worth it – the hardship is what defines us.

The gates rose and six dogs smashed their way past, the pounding of their paws on the wet-sand shaking through the floor below me. I saw the delight and determination in their eyes – the tunnel vision that pulled them forward so fast their tongues almost got left behind.

I'd always loved it, I realised. Why else was I here? I'd been driving around for days looking at wind-ravaged, rain-soaked beaches and points – but every bit of it was what I lived for.

Tomorrow, I knew we'd score. Because we deserved to. We'd put in the hours, the days. We'd shown the patience required.

My thoughts were broken by Rhyd yelling, running down the steps towards the finish line: 'Come on Number Five. Come on! You BEAUTY! Yes!'

He'd just won his three euros back.

A let-up in the rain ushered us on our way the next morning, back for the coasts of County Claire. A virtually empty N18 motorway took us up to Ennis, from where we dropped on to the country roads.

Here another squall washed over us from the west, blown in from the Atlantic, before another patch of weak sunlight brightened the swathes of green. At Ennistymon we turned to make a line straight for the coast, which appeared on the horizon almost immediately.

Clean, new-build houses lined the road – beach homes people had knocked up to enable themselves to retreat to the now not-so-wilds of western Claire for their holidays. Rhyd explained to me that the area was getting more and more built-up each year. The neatness and precision of a lot of the houses gave the place a quaint homeliness for now, most of the buildings wearing freshly rendered, coloured walls; yellows complimenting the youthful slate that had been deftly lined up along the roofs. More rain started to fall, this time at an angle suggesting the ocean winds were its driving force, and I wondered how much longer these homes would look so new.

For the tenth or more time this week we pulled up at Lahinch's beachfront promenade, and immediately I knew something had changed.

Waves were breaking hundreds of yards out to sea. A violent, unrelenting swell had finally built and burst after a week of storms out west. On the shoreline the white water was getting whipped by the wind so hard it was forming a thick foam, a couple of feet deep in places. The odd clump would then get picked up and roll, like tumbleweed in a Western, across the car park towards a boarded-up complex of beachfront amusement arcades and shops. Rhyd needed only one look at the ocean here to hatch a plan.

'We're going towards Spanish Point – somewhere round that neck of the woods'll be pumping in these conditions!'

We got back into his car and he drove out of Lahinch, but this time towards the south. The road steadily ascended from sea level, allowing us to check out the deeply embedded lines of swell powering their way into the bay below. About half a mile later, and with the ocean now well below us, the road suddenly swung inland and we were in farm country.

From here there were no signposts giving us a clue where to head and I was again grateful to have someone who knew this coastline driving me around. Rhyd started pointing out little side tracks and rocky outcrops, telling me what he thought of each one.

'I reckon there's a steaming left down there. Needs a really clean swell, though. No use today... Now see that big peninsula there – that's got the sickest slab you'll ever see breaking on the end of it some days. Too much for me, mind. Reckon it's one for the tow-in boys...'

The road had come back to being more level with the sea, as I spotted another promontory of rock up ahead. I could see waves all around the tip of it; two different peaks breaking at such differing angles that one was getting completely hammered by the wind, while the other was holding its shape invitingly. The only trouble with going out there was the size, as well as the fact that even at a couple of times overhead it still wasn't fully clearing the reef in front of it – certain death for the likes of us.

Eventually we rolled into the village of Spanish Point – so named because the place could lay claim to being the final resting place of some of the Spanish Armada vessels. A load of King Phillip's mariners had met grizzly ends here in a monumental storm, as a plaque outside the Armada Hotel informed us. Rhyd knew the rest of the story, which wasn't good news for the survivors either, apparently. They had waded ashore only to get executed anyway.

No sign of the wreckage could be seen today – although it was obvious from the moment we arrived that there were at least three quality surf spots if the conditions were right. A big, open-water reef break was raging away at the top of the point, while there was also a peak in front of the hotel that looked like it didn't quite have enough tide on it but was strangely immune to the wind. At the end of the road was a beach break, which several surfers were floundering around in. It looked ugly – big close-outs and little room to paddle or watch what was going on around you. A river was pouring thick brown water in from the south side of the beach, and I could see driftwood and farm effluent floating through the line-up. Looks were deceiving because, apart from the pigment given to it by local peat, this run-off was pollution-free and cleaner than anything you'd find at home.

We pulled up for a closer look. A lone surfer had stopped at the same time as us and was about to get back in his car when I called out to him for advice. This is often a risky move as local surfers can be very possessive, but he was nothing of the sort.

'That peak in front of the hotel is gonna work – round about now,' he explained. 'Pretty good too, I wouldn't mind betting. This beach break is a load of crap.'

We let him drive off and made our own way back towards the point to see if we could find a place to park.

It crossed our minds to leave the car at the hotel, but at home you'd get clamped for such a thing so just to be safe we made for a partially paved road that ran past a couple of secluded houses.

The exterior of the biggest house had been painted a ruby red that held my eye as we drove by. I craned my neck back to see if there were any signs of someone living there, before we went around a corner and the road plunged into the sea – literally. Part of the track had been washed away, but the bit where the landslide had occurred was now ideal for gaining access to the water's edge. Rhyd planted the car in a little verge of grass on the opposite side of the road and we stepped out to survey the surf.

Someone had just paddled out – maybe the guy we'd just talked to. Already the presence of a surfer had given us perspective. The waves were a lot bigger than they'd looked without anyone in the water and were bending in to form a little wedging wall. The wind still seemed not to be affecting it at all.

'That's odd,' I pointed out. 'The wind should be side shore, and it's still really gusty – how's this spot so clean?'

'Who cares? Let's get in there!'

We started suiting up. I was buzzing. Surf in Ireland, at last. Rhyd hid his key in the wheel-rim of the car – which you'd never do in Porthcawl because of thieves – and we slid our way off the break in the road, to the slimy rocks below.

Halfway out to the peak, I could see already why the surf was so clean. There were kelp plants a couple of feet long stuck to the bottom throughout the line-up. Kelp, besides giving an eerie feel to a place when it comes into view or swirls just below you, smoothes the water's surface and gives it an oily look. It helps keep waves clean when wind is trying to mess things up. It prevents the energy created by wind-chop from being able to resonate through the water and stops it from forming the mini-waves that break a longer-range swell up. Northern California is famous for its glassy, kelp-soothed waves, and right now it was a welcome discovery.

The swaying plants on the seabed were also making the waves 'boil'. This is when something unusually shallow beneath the wave causes water to upwell in front of it. It causes bumps and smaller lips to form in the middle of the face, kind of like steps that you need to negotiate as you ride. On take-off, a boil can have catastrophic effects, especially if it's a 'rock boil'.

As we arrived in the line-up Rhyd paddled for a wave, only to pull back when a whole series of boils appeared all the way down the line. This surf, I realised, was going to be a lot more intense than we'd been expecting. At this stage I was hoping that these were merely being caused by kelp. A rock boil would be a different proposition altogether.

There was a lot of water moving sideways through the line-up as well, and this meant that Rhyd was now well out of position. If another set swung through, it would catch him out and give him a good hiding.

That was exactly what happened. In fact, the set that came through next was so big that I had trouble getting out of its way even from the main take-off spot. I had to turn my back on Rhyd and paddle for the horizon.

The guy who'd paddled out ahead of us, meanwhile (who was not the same person we'd talked to on the beach), avoided all of the fuss with expertise – calmly paddling towards the channel the moment he'd spotted the waves feathering on the horizon. He then turned and headed back towards the impact zone just in time to catch the last one. From there his local experience only took him so far. A set of boils appeared, throwing him forward towards the trough and the kelp below. I had begun to feel like a wimp for not catching one myself, but now my decision seemed justified.

It took Rhyd so long to get out of the churning shallows that I had time to assess several waves before he made it outside again. On about the third or fourth attempt, I felt confident I'd found one I could successfully scratch my way over the ledge of.

The wave chucked me into a partially airborne drop, which caused my stomach to flop. I just made it intact and tried a tame, mid-face turn, only for the bottom to fall out of the wave. I felt my fins lose their grip and had to throw all of my weight to the back foot just to make it out on to the face again. Then the wave fizzled into deep water and I rode, heart racing, to the channel. The juice in these waves was no joke.

Two more surfers made their way into the line-up as we tried to get to grips with what was, for the moment, a ferocious reef break. I asked one of the other guys in the water how these conditions measured up to the usual Spanish Point experience.

'This is pretty good,' he said, looking upwards as if trying to invoke a memory from somewhere. 'Maybe a bit wonky, though. Too much tide already. But all the rain's filled the water with the soil run-off. It's made it all thick and syrupy and hard for the wind to blow out – look.' He lifted his hand and let the water run through his fingers.

You never know with a comment like this if it's based on something concrete – surfers are the world's best lay-scientists. But it made sense. The water did have a layered, Bovril-type colour – although when running through his fingers it looked more like weak tea. I watched a wave break. In the small spells of sunlight the roof of the lip looked almost yellowish. Combined with a landscape so drenched in green it meant the session was taking place with surroundings that were almost throbbing with colour.

I was getting slowly more confident with the take-off. The key was to lock in to the wave with as much paddle speed as you could build up, and to make sure you were well clear of the lip before jumping to your feet. Like Thurso East, or Up the Duff in the Hebrides, this was a wave that demanded total focus.

I was paddling back out from one of my more successful rides so far when Rhyd appeared at the crest of a set wave, poised to get into it. I yelled encouragement to him, seeing the suppressed excitement in his eyes as he focussed on the task at hand. Spreading his arms, crane-like, he kept the nose of his board high and then released himself for a freefall down to the bottom. I yelled again as he pulled the drop off and dug his inside rail in for a bottom turn. The tempo of this session was increasing with each wave.

Most of the time the peaks shifting through were warping and warbling too much to even think about the tube. I kept mind-surfing them on my way back out. Slowing enough to hook yourself in there, while still making it down the face, would be a risky business. But I couldn't help wondering what Jason Duffy, or Rhino and Jem, would have done here.

The one thing this wave was perfect for was swinging in to great, drawn-out cutbacks. A thick slope of heavy, cold, dark water is the surfing equivalent to several feet of powder on a snowboard, or a big, smooth tarmac slope to a skater. In fact, those other board sports have sprung up to *recreate* the sensation of surfing a wave like this. But nothing feels as pure as the real thing. To bury your board onto its edge and then throw all your weight through an arcing turn, knowing the water below will bear everything you throw at it, is a feeling of at-oneness with the ocean that rivals any tube ride.

If you timed it right, you could race away from the churning curl and then swing a full roundhouse turn all the way back to tag the foam ball just as it was ready to bounce you back on to the bowling wave face. Pulling that off from start to finish is something that embeds itself in your mind – so much so that recalling the memory of it can make you start twitching instinctively in all sorts of inappropriate landlocked situations: post office queues, restaurants, important meetings – even in the cinema with your feet resting on the chair in front.

Along with the aroma of sea, the ritual of creeping your way down across the slippery kelp and the first moment of contact with the sharp ocean, this was the intimate meeting with Ireland that I had wanted. When the tide rose, I made my way across the pebbles in front of the point with the trademark spring in my step of someone liberated by the power of surf stoke. I tiptoed across the lime-tinted moss and flat stones greased by liquid peat seeping out of the ground.

It was raining again, and I welcomed the fresh water pouring off the ocean from the now horizonless sky. The elements were making their way into my soul.

Rhyd caught a wave in too, and punched the air with both hands as he straightened out and made for the shore. Behind him two more locals continued to surf as the wind cranked itself up yet again. Did they realise how unique and how enviably blissful their experience of surfing was?

And did we?

Driving away, watching the car windows mist up from our wet hair, my mind wandered. The way the tube sections at Spanish Point had writhed and warped so unpredictably had reminded me a little of a couple of the reef breaks around West Wales – a place I should be starting to think more fondly of if I did feel the need to compete again.

I wondered how far I had to go before I was ready to make that call. Would next year's Welsh be a good chance to evaluate how far I'd come? And if so how would I judge that? Did it still matter? I wasn't sure any more if doing well there was still that important.

I began recalling the various times I'd exited early at the Welsh, thinking of the reasons behind it. Was it always my attitude? Did I deserve such rotten luck?

The narrowest loss of all had involved one of those rock boils, as it happened. Freshwater West, where the Welsh was usually held, had two contest sites. One was the main beach, on your right as you looked out to sea, while the other slightly more treacherous spot was known as Middle Bay. Middle Bay was surrounded by rising slopes of soft marram grass and topped with a high-vantage-point road lined with parking spaces, from where competitors could see across the coast for miles. The way the wave was situated at the foot of a staggered sitting area gave it this amphitheatre feel – you were often surrounded by spectators who were very close to the action. And yet while out there in a heat you were a world apart from them, struggling to find waves in conditions that were usually very taxing.

One of the main reasons for Middle Bay being considered so treacherous was a single, two-prong outcrop of rock that lurked close below the surface – known to the locals as 'Black Betty'. You never knew when Black Betty was going to show, which made catching the right wave a lottery. If you got lucky there'd be no sign at all, but on occasion a great cauldron of upwelling water would appear in front of the wave; as nasty a rock boil as any I knew. If Betty didn't actually protrude, her rock boil alone would be enough to bump you off, as the water below your board suddenly refused to do anything but swirl and bubble. It was an aquatic version of quicksand, pulling you down for a closer inspection of the unforgiving reef.

One year I was picked on by Betty during my round two heat. By accident, she helped me get one of the waves of the event – although even that wasn't enough to assist in my ill-fated plight. I had dropped in unaware of her presence, only to see her pop up right in front of me. Steering down the face to avoid having to drink my food through a straw for the next month, I found a part of the wave that was unaffected – whereupon with no warning the remnants of Betty's boil caused a tube to throw forward. Without really doing anything to deserve it, I was suddenly lodged behind a curtain of water, still holding enough rail in the wave to keep my line. As often happens in the tube, instinct took over, and a moment later I was out, racing back towards safety. The score I got was unusually high for the conditions. The judges hadn't been expecting anything of the sort that morning, and it left me needing to do little more than get to my feet on a second wave to make it to the next round with a solid performance under my belt.

There are probably few surfers in Wales capable of spending ten minutes failing to catch a half-decent wave in clean Middle Bay with only three others out – but I was one of them. Even Black Betty coming to my aid hadn't been enough to break my Welsh Nationals hoodoo.

Black Betty was, of course, infamous in Welsh surfing lore. Several plots had been mooted over the years to dynamite the offending lump of limestone by night – but aside from the time she helped add another failed nationals campaign to my collection, I also had a very fond memory of Pembroke's renegade rock boil.

One of my and Rhyd's best friends in school, Tristan, used to invite us on surf trips to Fresh West with his dad, Geoff. Geoff Davies was, along with my father, one of the early legends of Porthcawl surfing, and hailed from a day when travelling over Wales and England usually made up the largest part of any surfer's lifetime itinerary. Theirs was a generation that certainly had the stoke needed to keep surfing enthusiastically in British waters, and on these trips we'd often meet other members of the old guard.

Geoff used to 'rescue' us from school. On one of the hottest days I can recall, he and my dad had left messages for the receptionist to come and get us, citing family emergencies. Smugly, we walked free from our geography class, knowing exactly what the emergency was.

A lined-up, three-foot summer swell was hitting Middle Bay, almost every wave hitting Black Betty at exactly the right angle to tube over her without too much disruption. Two of my dad and Geoff's mates, both of whom have since sadly, passed away, were out enjoying the session, revelling in the sweet conditions on offer below skies utterly clear of cloud. One was Paul Ryder, one of the founding fathers of Welsh surfing, whose thin face with its short beard and wise eyes was then one of the most regular in the Fresh West line-up. Another was Jeff Price, the wetsuit maker, who wore a permanent smile whenever I saw him.

We'd enjoyed a whole day of surfing, and now the tide was dropping below the reef at Middle Bay as the sun fell low in the sky. My dad, Tristan and I, and the two local legends were sitting on that elevated grass verge – the selfsame amphitheatre in which I'd have a very different experience years later – and watching the lines roll through. Geoff Davies was looking for a wave in, and found one. There was something odd about it though, and after a few turns we all gasped as we realised it would run past Black Betty. At this lower stage of tide the rock was so defined you could see its two slightly separate peaks – and it was the gap between these that Geoff chose as the route to safety. Others on the hill also started whooping as he lined up to shoot through the rocks – a passage so narrow a surfboard would only make it if its trajectory was inch-perfect.

Crouching into 'hero stance' Geoff took aim and flew through the two rocks, while the watching crowd erupted. For all the noise they could just as easily have been watching the winning goal in a football match.

As the oldies crowded him and offered their praise, Geoff stated matter-of-factly: 'I've wondered if that was possible for years, and when I got that wave just then I thought it had the right amount of water in front of it and thought, fuck it, let's give it a go!'

Tristan's face dropped. Not only had his dad just pulled off one of the most heroic surfing stunts he'd ever seen – but he'd *sworn* too! We were slowly being inducted into their world, and we loved it.

These were the memories I should be holding onto of Middle Bay, of Fresh West, I thought. What did losing in a drizzly contest matter anyway?

Mind you, in Ireland you could even learn to love drizzle – with a bit of meditative mind control.

I wondered if thinking about the Welsh Nationals as any kind of objective for me wasn't just a bit crass – sure it had been where this idea to get out and about within the UK, and now Ireland too, had begun germinating, but did that really matter now? Jeff Davies's approach to Black Betty was infinitely more memorable than mine. It was legendary, and he hadn't needed a contest vest, an affiliation fee, a disclaimer, a stopwatch. He hadn't been surfing to the hoot of a horn. Surfing was about the pursuit of freedom anyway, wasn't it?

As well as the waiting.

For this visit to Ireland, short and sweet though its eventual payload had been, the wait had been worthwhile. The rain, the cabin fever – it had been rewarded.

'I suppose in the end it was better that we had to wait almost a week for that,' I noted to Rhyd, as he turned the wipers up again to fend off another encroaching belt of rain. 'You kind of feel as if you deserve it when you've put something in.'

He didn't say anything for a moment, as if he had to think about it. But then he asked, 'What's that play with those two blokes who wait for nothing to happen? They're Irish aren't they? Come on, you ought to know.'

'D'you mean *Waiting for Godot*?'

'Yeah. I think so. Don't they just wait and wait, and then it turns out they're waiting for something that doesn't exist?'

'Kind of.'

'That's cool,' he said, moving his attention from the wiper dials to the windscreen heaters. 'Don't you reckon? I think it's awesome. That's us, isn't it. Two guys driving around a desolate landscape searching for I-don't-know-what, and then kind of thinking we might be there, but only for an afternoon. Isn't the wait the thing that gives a surfer's life meaning, anyway?'

'Yeah, it is, I suppose. Or if not the wait, it's the search at least.'

'So what about surfers then?' Rhyd asked. 'Aren't they waiting for something that doesn't exist?'

'I dunno. Maybe. Do you think it exists?'

Rhyd paused, turning the dial on the radio back down. He thought for a moment and then answered firmly:

'Yes. I think it does. Yes. It does exist.'

CHAPTER 13

CEREDIGION ON NEW YEAR'S DAY, AND RAINBOW'S END

*I*t does exist.

I should have known all along. Or rather remembered, because commitment and belief are two of the fundamental pillars of the surfing religion. To really score you need faith that what you're after is out there somewhere, and above all you must make some kind of sacrifice.

OK, so I'd sacrificed plenty of time and money in the last year, sanity in Ireland, honesty in my industrial backyard, sleep in Scotland and my body's core temperature all over the place. But I'd never imagined this one coming. And neither had my drinking buddies...

'You what? *Staying in on New Year's Eve?*'

'Yep. I'm not feeling too good, like. Getting a bit over the New Year thing, in my old age and all. I fancy giving it a miss this time.' I'd been repeating this, or something to the same effect, for days.

The reality was that my friend Jean (nicknamed so because he hated France) had spotted a once-a-decade swell making its way towards Cardigan Bay at an angle that might spark a rare gem into breaking, and he'd cooked up a plan to hit it at the dawn of the New Year, along with Breige and me.

From the moment it was suggested, I knew we were onto something epic. The deviousness I had employed to hide this plan was so far-reaching that I even lied on the radio the morning before. For a while now I'd occasionally gone in to talk about the contents of the newspapers on Radio Wales's breakfast-time show, and being nowhere near important enough to ever turn down a gig (unlike one of their other paper reviewers it seems), I had accepted a last-minute request to go in and do just that on New Year's Eve. With most of the world asleep and uninterested in following the news, this was, barring some hideous unforeseen event, the slowest news day possible – so before long the presenter, Sarah Dickins, and I had run out of topics.

'So what are you doing to celebrate tonight then, Tom?' she asked.

Suddenly caught out by a googly of a question, I mumbled, 'Uh, er…'

In the virtual spotlight of the studio, I froze. All eyes looked across at my lonely corner of the table and Sarah lifted an earphone to prompt a quicker response. Silence on the radio is poison. It was a straightforward question, I knew, but I hadn't anticipated it. I could hardly tell the nation that my real New Year plans were to sneak before daybreak up to mid-Wales to try and catch one of the most elusive surf spots in the British Isles, and that I had heard on good authority it was threatening to break as good as it ever got on the morrow.

But vanity can get the better of you when the media are stroking your ego and to get the skit up and running again I blurted out, 'Cocktail party – at my place. Some friends are coming around. Should be a good one.'

'Ooh – what time?' asked Sarah.

'Er, seven-thirty. Come along if you want!'

'Maybe I will,' came the reply, in jest. 'Is that an open invite to all our listeners?'

I wondered if she could tell I was squirming. Safe to say, I spent the rest of the afternoon dodging phone calls about the party that wasn't.

Just under twenty-four hours later, feeling snidely superior to the rest of the human race, we were loading boards into Jean's van to drive through the dark on one of the coldest nights of the winter towards our destination.

January has a bite to it that surfers feel perhaps more acutely than anyone else in Britain. It is a time of year when the sun that we usually worship is so far gone, so long lost, that it feels as if our part of the planet has been dipped into the sub-zero abyss of outer space. At night, when an easterly wind blows, a jet of water can be frozen before it hits a windscreen. The cold doesn't want you to surf. It tries to get in through any gap you give it. Before you get in the water it looks to creep in through the bottom of your coat, up your trouser legs, around your scarf. If you give it a naked hand it'll seize it and turn that smallest of appendages against you.

And in the midst of these icy winds from the frozen continent to our east, we were planning to try and get into wetsuits and submerge ourselves in a sea that wasn't much warmer than the air it had been chilled by.

But it was all about the sacrifice. The bigger the sacrifice, the bigger the gain. We were, after all, on the tail of one of the best waves in the land.

Where exactly that wave lies, again, is something I could only print if I had a death wish – but I can tell you that the wave was a long, fast-breaking left point, that I will dub 'Pavones' due to its uncanny resemblance to the Costa Rican wave of the same name. Pavones had always held an uncomfortable place in my heart after I was forced to watch Breige surf it for a week whilst my leg was in plaster years before. I'd returned to Pavones two years later, to see to unfinished business, and it had left me with a lifelong love of fast left-hand point breaks. The thought that one existed in Wales was something I'd been losing sleep over long before this restless New Year's Eve. A challenge had been set, and I was going to surf the Welsh Pavones at any cost.

It was all a routine to me now, a routine I loved – one that I had become completely addicted to – the buzz sitting up-front in the van as we waited for that first glimpse of coastline. The roads were lined with ice and even the odd patch of snow as we crawled through the higher parts of Carmarthenshire. Jean was trying to get hold of the sage-like Gower longboarder, known as 'Guts', with his mobile and was getting no response. A promising sign.

Guts (real name Chris Griffiths) was another longboarder and one of the Welsh surfers, along with Elliot Dudley, to have really made an impact on the international scene. A veteran traveller, both he and his photographer mate Paul Gill (known, unimaginatively as 'the Gill') were formidably knowledgeable surf-spot buffs. If they were headed somewhere and you found out about it – which would be rare as they were pretty secretive about where they turned up – then it was as good a tip as you could ever hope for. The Gill would show up at my local breaks only on the biggest, cleanest days imaginable – and seeing him arrive on the beach would always send a chill up your spine. His presence indicated you were surfing the finest waves in Wales, or even further, that day.

One of the main factors leading us to call this trip 'on' last night had been Jean's inability to reach Guts on the phone. Jean worked with Guts, fixing the surfboards he made ('Guts Surfboards' – again a creative name), and had been talking to him a few days earlier about the possibility of Pavones breaking on New Year's Day. Guts had been in a particularly friendly mood, perhaps brought on by the Yuletide spirit, and hadn't ruled the rumour out. Guts mentioning that he thought one of the classic surf spots of legend might be about to work, only to then go off the radar, could only mean one thing.

'You know it's gonna be pumpin' when he gets all cagey about where he's going surfing,' Jean explained, as the first hints of sunrise started appearing in the wing mirrors. Patches of black ice had covered most of the roads on the way up, causing us to make much slower progress than we'd hoped. Grit stocks had been waning after a Christmas period of frequent freezing temperatures. Any patches of water that had got caught in the cold blast had turned rock hard, stuck sorrowfully in place like corpses of puddles.

We didn't want sunrise. That would mean waves were going to waste.

However much we wished darkness to stick around, though, it couldn't hold off forever, and dawn had begun to break by the time we made it on to the mid-Wales coastal highway. An ominously clear, starry night gave way to a rising winter sun – and rigid lines of swell, stacked to the horizon and groomed by the biting winds. Tiny ribs of offshore wind brushed their way over the top of each wave, as they steadily rose out of the ocean behind a reef break breaking on the edge of a small, beach-side town, the name of which I will never be able to give you. Jean was highlighting this as an indication for what to expect at our own, top-secret destination.

A blazing yellow sun had now raised enough to dip behind the dark grey clouds that hung above the horizon. There was moisture in the air – although the likelihood had to be that it would snow before raining. Sure enough, flakes began floating from the air above us as we paused at a rise in the road. A lay-by offered a view of the coast for miles in each direction. Whether due to snow, sleet or low-lying cloud, a rainbow had formed a few miles along the coast.

'Fuckin' end of it's right where we're going!' Jean marvelled. 'It's pointin' to where Pavones is an' all!' His voice struggled to hide how overwhelmed he was.

We hopped back in and pulled onto the road. I peered at his speedometer. It had started creeping steadily up. This was a chase now.

'Better blindfold yourselves in a minute,' he joked, before turning off without indicating. 'Not sure *I* even want you to know where this place is.'

The road he'd picked had a 'no access' sign. This was private property but, before we could ask, Jean explained there was an 'unspoken agreement' in place with surfers.

'We'll be there in less than a minute now,' he said, shakily. 'And it's gonna be the best surf you've ever seen in Wales.'

After a build-up line like that, I hoped he could deliver.

He could. Seconds later all his talking-up of the surf that awaited us had been thoroughly vindicated.

The narrow road ahead suddenly stopped at a shoreline of round boulders. The first indication that the pot of gold existed was there before us: a long-wheelbase van with 'Guts Surfboards' emblazoned on its flank and two smaller, older vans next to it. A yellow commercial Astra and a red Transit. Behind these was one other vehicle: a white camper parked a little off the road.

'That's the Gill's,' Jean whispered, reaching below his steering column to pull the hand brake up. My heart missed a beat. We had stumbled on a clandestine gathering of surf legends – this was indeed Rainbow's End.

The three of us, Jean, Breige and I all jumped out of the van and ran through a row of beached boats to the edge of the point. Four left-handers, each well over a hundred yards long, were chugging in unison down the boulder-reef, thick lips spilling down the line with a rhythmic, mechanical movement. As a fifth wave arrived at the point I saw a thick-built longboarder in a silver wetsuit glide into a take-off, drawing a low line around the first two sections, before going in to a carve at the first opportunity and setting up a straight-line dash towards where we were standing. It was Guts.

We didn't need to watch it for another second. The desire to be in the water, to be ourselves hooking into one of these grinding, endless waves, was almost too strong even to get our wetsuits on. The Siberian winds vanished in our minds, no longer any kind of obstacle to our throwing layers of soaking neoprene on. Frost-hardened turf underfoot meant nothing. Grey skies or blue, water at six degrees or twenty-six, the only thing that mattered was the surf – a world-class, racing point break, firing directly in front of us.

Getting ready passed in a flash – but treading across the rocks to the water's edge took an eternity. Holding my board against the wind, it was simply something you couldn't do quickly enough. Each pool and barnacle needed to be carefully stepped over, or through, with care. To try and run would result in going head over heels and slipping over a boulder. But with surf good enough to corrupt any thought pattern right in front of you the whole time, it was hard to focus. Patience was trying its best to desert me.

Halfway up to the stream at the top of the point that looked the best place to paddle out, I saw the Gill, crouching and peering through a 600 mm lens.

'All right,' he said softly, from within a raised duffel hood. His black moustache masked his lips, so you could barely make out what he was saying. 'Looks good out there. You're late.'

'Late? It's been light for about twenty minutes!'

'Yep. Guts and Kook have had some screamers already.' He cut off to train his camera at the line-up. A slender natural-foot with black graffiti on the deck of his board hopped up and rose fluidly across a standing wall of green wave face, kinking his back knee in to his body as he finally descended to the bottom and took aim, looking for somewhere to connect with the lip. As he threw spray out of the back of the wave, the Gill's camera whirred. This was Mark Jones, one of Swansea's hottest underground surfers – who had been nicknamed 'Kook' since I'd first known him. In the water he was anything but that. By the time he'd hit his fifth turn we were watching the ride from the back. Kook had gone so far down the point as to pass us completely.

'You're next,' Gill said, raising an eyebrow. 'Get in there'.

I waded out to my thighs with Breige and Jean alongside me, and then the three of us jumped into the prone position and paddled as fast as we could for the line-up. The waves were running down the point at such an angle that it was easy to slip out between them, and all three of us got into position with our hair still dry under thick wetsuit hoods. From the little bits of wind spray that had caught my face, I could tell the sea temperature was bordering on lethal. The only skin I had left exposed, my cheeks and forehead, were already burning with cold.

There would be little let-up from the ice cream headaches if any of us got caught in front of a set, because waves were coming through pretty much constantly.

Paddling out I'd expected to drift down the point a bit, as so many waves churning their way along a shore in the same direction normally create a rip, but this hadn't happened so I was still quite a way behind the part of the wave that looked best. The Gill was now fifty yards further down the line, and the first part of the wave seemed fast and hard to keep up with. Thinking it preferable to paddling along the point though, I figured I'd catch one and see how far it could get me.

I took off on a wave that was only just over waist-high and concentrated on streamlining my backhand stance as best I could, angling my shoulders to get tight and place myself in the high point of the lip line. Squeezing all the momentum I could find from my board, I revved as far ahead of it as possible. With that bitter wind flying up the face, you could feel the smooth speed of a powerful wave beneath your feet. A little along the section it occurred to me that I may well make it through to the main corridor after all, and that the wave was actually growing in size as it reeled along. By the time I'd raced around onto an invitingly stacked shoulder, I'd become completely consumed by the glide. Each time I aimed a turn at the top of the wave it would jack-up and I'd need to cut the turn off, crouch and fly along another section. Kook passed by on his way back out and cheered at me as I dropped back down to find the wall now well over my head. Right across the bay in front of me I could see water drawing in, pulled by the energy of what I was riding. And still it raced on. Eventually, as a thumping close-out primed itself before me, I aimed all my speed at the pitching section, floating weightless across it and landing with a jerk that caused my knees to crumple. With all my senses on overdrive, I was ready for the impact and rode out. I jumped back to my stomach and turned for a little concrete slipway, having just ridden for such a distance that it was going to take several minutes to walk back.

Drawing a deep breath, oxygen and adrenaline both met and collided inside my body and I let out a shriek to acknowledge a ride that rivaled anything I'd ever experienced before.

'Yeeeaaaah! This is sick! SICK!'

I ran back to the grass, to the pathway up the point. I wanted to yell. To tell someone. I wanted another one.

'Did you see that?' I screamed at the Gill as I cantered past him, this time seemingly immune to the risk of slipping on the rocks.

'That was nothing,' he shot back at me coolly.

Bristling with impatience, I waded out closer to the middle of the point this time. It meant having to duck-dive, and I could feel my head contracting. I arrived in the line-up holding my temples and wincing, but was immediately distracted. It was Kook's turn to fly past me on a bomb. A born showman, he kinked off the bottom right where I was and aimed a bucket right for me. His fins swooshed through the green, see-through rear of the wave as he dropped back down and prepared to enter the racetrack himself.

This wave was so flawless you could get a buzz simply from seeing someone else ride it.

That was illustrated perfectly on the next set, when in front of a rolling mound of white water I spotted a few surfers scrambling to get out the way. The biggest wave yet was coming through and at the top of the point it had crumbled across the line-up. One of the surfers managed to latch onto the avalanche and get to their feet. They stood up, waiting for the wave to adjust itself and hit the main strait as hard and fast as a solid set might do in any of the world's finest breaks. The surfer held on as the wave began to topple and then I spotted the white deck and pink rails of a very recognisable board. It was Breige.

I was one of several surfers hooting at her as she began to tear across a wave well over twice her height. It was a wave shaped to drag you to delirium, and as she whizzed past I could hear the lip crashing across the trough below. It sounded like a peal of thunder tearing through the atmosphere. My head turned to watch the back of the wave, but so much water was getting lifted off it by the wind that it rained for a few seconds, by which time she was already past the spot where Kook had kicked out. She'd have a long walk herself now, too.

What made these waves so supremely suited to surfing was the way that such an awesome display of the ocean's power had been harnessed to move with such precision. The raw force of the swell was transferring into a source of power that seemed tailor-made for a surfboard. Each wave would give you the feeling you were burrowing into something special as you stroked over the ledge. The faces were so smooth you could jump to your feet while angling for the ride ahead. Beneath you would then be all the fuel you needed to turn wherever you wanted to go. To move, react to and interact with such speed, derived from no source other than the natural movement of the ocean, was a feeling of purest freedom. Ruler-straight lines of water were stacking up behind the point over and over – each of these waves a blank canvas. Every time you took off it was in the knowledge that almost 500 yards of pure pleasure lay ahead, in which you made the rules and nobody else.

On top of this, I had run a headcount of the line-up. We were sharing this nirvana with only ten other surfers. Half the waves were left unridden – to grind along without intervention from humankind. Seeing these waves as you hopped back along the rocks to paddle out again fed the imagination. It helped you marvel at where *you* might be, if that had been your next ride. It loosened the mind ready for when, liberated of any worry other than riding perfect waves, you next dropped in.

And that moment was never far away.

Animals in the wild may feed until they pass out, as they don't know when they may get the next chance. In that sense, it can be said they share something with surfers. Like I'd done in Thurso, and so many other places when you know you're riding waves that will thrill you for the rest of your life, you shut out thoughts of cold, of hunger, fatigue – anything that may stand in your way. This was one of those sessions where you'd keep going until either you, or the waves, ceased to function.

With toes that no longer belonged to my own nervous system, a lower back frozen to where it might as well have fused, lips blistering from the salt and ruthless sub-zero winds, a stomach hungry enough to begin digesting itself and shoulders ready to drop off, we kept surfing.

Three hours in, I'd begun weighing up what this session may mean. As we whiled away the winter morning, ignoring the need to stop surfing, I tried to hold on to the moment once again. I needed to guard it in my subconscious – a keepsake. This was what the last year had been building towards. The unadulterated joy of surfing at home. Mid-winter had done nothing to shake off that love. I'd come through in the end. My status as a fully-hooked British surfer had finally returned once and for all.

When the tide did finally release us all from the spell of the Welsh Pavones, it was left to the two we'd indirectly followed down here to sum it up.

First the Gill wandered over to Jean's van as the three of us tried to pack our stuff back up. With the wind still slashing its way down to us from across the rest of the freezing country, it was a labour to pause and talk to anyone. But this was the Gill, and he looked as if he had something meaningful to say.

'Nice wave you had earlier,' he nodded to Breige. 'I've, er, racked my brain, and I think that's the best wave I've ever seen a girl ride. Outside of Hawaii, of course.'

This was a conversation killer that nobody seemed to mind. It was all he had to say, beyond wishing us well, and we watched him stroll away.

Jean ran the van up past Guts, who was also loading his board up for the drive back to Swansea, and wound the window down to say bye.

'All right? Bet Porthcawl was all right today,' Guts quipped.

'Yeah.' I couldn't tell if he was joking. 'Wind wouldn't be any use, though.'

I tried to quiz him briefly about the spot. I wanted to know just how good we'd scored it and how often it broke. I already knew, deep down, that it was unlikely I'd surf this place again like this for years, if ever. Guts didn't need to say anything to put me off trying to come back with a crew from back home. It wasn't necessary to fabricate tales of how rarely this wave appeared, to try to convince me of its elusive, enigmatic status. The truth would be enough.

'What can I say?' he barked, opening his arms out to an emphatic shrug. 'You could come here a hundred times and never see it like that again. This is one of the luckiest days of your surfing life. Remember these waves well. Ride them over in your head. It won't happen again. Not for a long, long time anyway.'

A second, equally satisfying conversation killer.

The best bit about a session like the one we'd just had is that you can indeed do that. Not only is it easy to run the waves through in your mind, it's addictive. This session would be distracting me and drawing me to daydream through all kinds of situations in the future. The changes these waves had made to our moods would last days, weeks. In years to come I'd be able to lift my spirits by recalling some of the sets I'd caught at Pavones today.

'Let's swing into the town that can't be named, get a hot broth from the main hotel and then go home to die,' Jean suggested, as he flipped his indicator on and waited for a chance to pull out on to the main road again. It was all part of the routine: sliding back in to the main stream of traffic, falling in line – putting the enormity of where we'd just been that little further behind us.

There were no objections to his proposal. It would keep us that little bit closer to the experience for perhaps an hour longer. We were all cold to the core by now and would need the energy anyway for the ride home.

'I'll be more wrecked today than if we'd stayed out all night partying,' I gloated.

'Typical New Year's Day feeling then, eh?' said Breige.

'For me, normally, today would have been all about a hangover and nothing else,' Jean mused. 'But good to have a change this year…'

'Are we gonna tell anyone where we were then?' I asked.

'At some point. I'll have to. Can't keep a sesh like that a secret forever. Telling people's half the reason you go, innit.'

'But let's not say just yet,' I suggested. 'Keep it to ourselves for now. It'll be kind of cool to see the evening of New Year's Day in with the same drained, chill-out mood as everyone else. Except our heads'll be fried for reasons known only to us.'

'Deal,' said Jean. Breige laughed.

'So if anyone speaks to me tonight,' I confirmed. 'I'll just say I knackered myself at the cocktail party. You can be my alibis. I mean, you two were there anyway, weren't you?'

POSTSCRIPT

'Where were you yesterday afternoon, man? You missed it! Middle Bay was firing, and Ianto got pummelled by Black Betty. And I mean *pummelled*! He ended up climbing the bigger rock on the inside, man. Like a flippin' mountaineer – with his board hanging off the end of his leash. It was like Flea done that time at Mavericks in all the mags – remember?'

I was back at the Welsh Nationals. And it was day two. I'd had to do a double-take myself, but it had happened. Day two. I had finally advanced through some heats.

The best bit though, was that it had happened in a new category: the seniors. It may sound a bit overly honourable a name for a category that simply required you to be twenty-eight or more on 1 January, but I was proud enough. I was on for a piece of silverware at last. As well as at least three weeks out of the water once this was done. I had ibuprofen to thank as much as anything for my progress.

Maybe it was the impact of entering something called 'seniors', but whatever the category lacked in rusty limbs and decrepit journeymen had been more than made up for by my antics. After getting dunked out of the Open as usual, I hadn't held out much hope for my first foray into this new world of the more elderly surfer, especially when I drew the same guy I'd just lost to in the main event.

But this time, stoked just to be here, a much more content me had headed down to the water's edge looking forward to a heat in fun, low-tide peaks. On the way another surfer in my heat, Greg Owen – who lived about a hundred yards from me in Porthcawl – was telling me how one of our friends had gotten into a spot of bother with Black Betty during yesterday afternoon's proceedings. I'd missed it, having gone for a surf myself. As I said, I was here for the crack now. Competing was just a secondary consequence. My outlook had become irrepressibly positive.

Until I'd jumped over the shore break two minutes later, and noticed a popping feeling behind one of my lower ribs. Immediately my right shoulder seized up and I winced with pain. I'd done my back in before the heat had even begun.

Still believing it might paddle off, I floundered my way into the line-up, moaning the whole time. Greg later said he thought it was a mind trick. (As if I'd care for that nonsense these days.)

I could see why he thought it, though. With five minutes left, and not having caught anything of use, I decided to call it a day – and paddled for the first wave that would take me to shore. An innocuous left-hander trickled through and I stood up; only to find myself pain-free and looking at a beautifully lined-up wall. Seven turns later I realised I'd fluked my way, via injury, into a big score. The pain returned as soon as I tried to paddle but, even so, this time I wasn't going to make my favourite mistake. Gasping for breath, and minimising shoulder movement, I struggled another twenty yards back out to sea and stood up on a small right-hander, which reformed in to the shore break and allowed me to do two small manoeuvres. When I limped back to the car it was to the news I'd sneaked through to the next round.

An hour of immense fuss followed as a volunteer physio from Christian Surfers (who were helping run the event out of the kindness of their hearts) checked me out.

'Nothing serious,' he confirmed. 'It's probably just a popped rib. Wrap up now and go home if you want to surf again in a few days. Otherwise take loads of painkillers, keep it cold, and you'll make it through the event – just. The time out'll be longer, mind – more like a couple of weeks – but it's your decision.'

I looked at the heat draw, at my name in fresh ink in one of the next round's heats, and opted for a bit of mind over matter.

Twenty-four hours, several boxes of pills and a few heats later I was in the final.

Although this was an achievement to toast for sure, there were still a few comfortingly self-depreciating statistics looming over me to place it into context. The last final I'd made at the Welsh was exactly a decade before, and also in an age-restricted sub-division. As an eighteen-year-old I'd made the final of the juniors, before having to fend for myself against the real grown-ups in the Open for years to come. That had been the point from which I'd embarked on my wonderful losing streak. But now this losing streak, which I had almost grown affection for, had ended with my eligibility at long last for one of the age-biased categories.

'Welcome to the gentlemen's event,' another competitor had said, smiling warmly. 'You're old enough now. None of those aggro kids – just us wise old guys, chilling and surfing together, with a couple of trophies up for grabs as an afterthought.'

He wasn't exaggerating either. As I tried to ignore the pain in my back for one more heat, I was aware that the emphasis was no longer anywhere near trying to prove your prowess. This was about like-minded surfers, who wanted a reason to drive out west one weekend, getting together for a bit of a surf-off. Coming out of heats, your opponent would say things like 'That was fun, eh?', rather than frowning and running off to get warm for the next round.

The best bit about all of this was how obvious the lessons of the past year had suddenly become. This, I realised, was no different to any of the other jaunts I'd embarked upon in the past twelve months. I'd suddenly seen this hallowed event for exactly what it was: a surf trip. Nothing more; nothing less. And one that drew a community of kindred spirits together. It was an excuse. A catalyst. A rendezvous.

My problem had been a complete failure to recognise that. I'd been going to the Welsh with nothing to give back. Ashamed of any attempts to celebrate surfing in a corner of the world I'd come to see as a non-starter of a surf destination, it was no wonder I'd been reaping what I'd sown. I shuddered to think why on earth I'd thought I was coming down here if it wasn't for the satisfaction of wanderlust, or to catch up with friends who pursued the same road to who-knows-where. For a dreaded moment it crossed my mind that it could have even been vanity, insecurity, a desire to prove myself. But then I realised that I'd never really known my reason for coming here. Maybe I hadn't even had one. At least I'd been true to myself in that much. That was fine, I thought. I'd gotten a bit lost. That was all. Nothing wrong with that.

And anyway, if that hadn't happened, there'd never have been a journey. It was healthy to get lost once in a while.

Strapping my leash on to paddle into the clear waters of Pembroke's most famous beach, I thought about my game plan. It was simple enough. Even through the ibuprofen, my slightly wiser backbone was telling me this was the last go-out for a little while. There would be time to sit back, recuperate and reflect. But for now, that could wait. There were waves to ride and the me of today was going to enjoy them on behalf of the me that would exist in the next few weeks. I knew I'd be thanking myself for it.

I smirked, wondering what the me of last year would make of this. Tough shit. He had no say any more. He really hadn't had a clue. But it was OK. The me of right now was willing to smile about it. I forgave myself – as long as the promise was made never to fall into that trap again.

OTHER TITLES BY TOM ANDERSON:

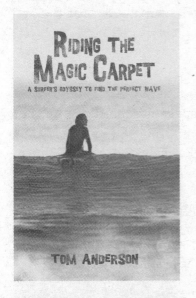

Riding the Magic Carpet

ISBN: 978-1-84024-502-8   £9.99

Jeffrey's Bay, South Africa – the fantasy, the almost mythical waves every surfer dreams of riding once in their lifetime. But Tom wouldn't go until he was ready. He would seek out surf spots from the virgin reef breaks of the Outer Orkneys to the temple point breaks of Indonesia, from the beautiful beaches of France to the wilds of Sri Lanka, a secret cove in Panama and a reflective spell in Costa Rica, all on a quest to ride the waves of his dreams.

Chasing Dean

ISBN: 978-1-84024-741-1   £9.99

Two childhood friends from small-town Wales meet in Miami for a summer road trip they've always dreamed of: to chase a hurricane swell along the US East Coast in search of the perfect wave. Giving themselves to the whim of Hurricane Dean leads to once-in-a-lifetime surf and a chance to reflect on their chosen paths. As the pair journey all the way up the Eastern Seaboard, they embark on a hilarious journey of self-discovery and a travel experience like no other.

Have you enjoyed this book? If so, why not write a review on your favourite website?

Thanks very much for buying this Summersdale book.

www.summersdale.com